D1071402

NOW WE ARE CIVILIZED

Charles M. Leslie

Assistant Professor
Department of Sociology and Anthropology
Pomona College

Now We Are Civilized

A Study of the World View
of the Zapotec Indians
of Mitla, Oaxaca

DETROIT · WAYNE STATE UNIVERSITY PRESS · 1960

*Grateful acknowledgment is
made to the Ford Foundation
for financial assistance in
the publication of this volume.*

ERRATUM

*Under illustration facing page 16,
for "wealthier" read "poorer."*

*Copyright © 1960. All Rights Reserved
Wayne State University Press. Detroit 2, Michigan
Library of Congress Catalog Card Number 60-7651*

Acknowledgments

I thank the Mitleños, too numerous to name individually, who graciously welcomed us into their homes and made our stay in their community a pleasant and genuinely educational experience.

It is too late now to thank Professor Robert Redfield, who made our research possible. I grieve his death.

My wife, Zelda Leslie, and Professor Morton Cronin have been patient collaborators. Professor Cronin edited most of the manuscript, giving me valuable lessons in ways to achieve clarity of expression. I am also grateful to Drs. Sol Tax, E. Adamson Hoebel, Gottfried Lang, Melvin Seiden, Robert Hinshaw, and Alvin Scaff, with whom I discussed various problems which arose in the process of writing this book. Professor Raymond Firth helpfully commented on some of the material in Chapter I, which I presented to a seminar on social change, of which he and Professor Redfield were co-chairmen, at the University of Chicago. I have followed his suggestion for a title to the whole work. Professor Julian Pitt-Rivers kindly suggested several editorial changes, which have been incorporated in the present text, and Professor Eric Wolf helped me with suggestions for the Appendix.

Mr. and Mrs. E. R. Frissell entertained us on many occasions at their home in Mitla. We went to market in Oaxaca in their automobile, and on such holidays as Thanksgiving, Christmas and Easter we enjoyed with them a home away from home.

v

Dr. Santiago Barahona S. guarded our health, and became our close friend while we were in Mitla. Miss Eleanor Briggs courteously helped us in the Zapotec language. In addition, during our stay in Mexico we enjoyed the hospitality and good advice of Professors Julio de la Fuente, Alfonso Villa Rojas, Fernando Cámara B., and Calixta Guiteras. I am most grateful to them.

Finally, I thank the Haynes Foundation, which provided funds to complete the present manuscript; the Department of Anthropology of the University of Chicago, whose initial grant made our research possible; and the Ford Foundation, whose funds we received through the program for the comparative study of cultures and civilizations directed by Professors Robert Redfield and Milton Singer.

C.M.L.

Introduction

Robert Redfield has defined world view as "an arrangement of things looked out upon, things in the first instance conceived of as existing. It is the way the limits or 'illimits,' the things to be lived with, in, or on, are characteristically known." As Redfield observed, the concept of world view is one of those inclusive concepts, like that of culture, or ethos, or national character, which refer to "aspects of the totality of group character." [1] Further:

> World view does not start from any choice of a particular segment of cultural life. It does not emphasize economy or personality or even ethos, system of moral norms. It enters seriously into the possibility of devising a form of thought for general use of the real whole of the little community that awaits the insider's total vision and conception of everything. [2]

This is so much more than what we have accomplished that our subtitle might better be "Studies in the World View of the Zapotec Indians of Mitla, Oaxaca," or, abandoning the term "world view" altogether, "A Study of the Zapotec Indians. . . ." Yet our purpose in going to Mitla was to learn about the world view of the townspeople, and what we have written is a record of our more significant findings.

There were aspects of "the insider's total vision and conception of everything," which we learned very little about. For example, we suppose that the members of most societies develop some characteristic conceptions of and feelings about their bodies and that the way they see the self and the rest of the world is somehow mediated by a "body image." But in order to comprehend this aspect of their world view we would have had to pursue much further than we had the time to do, a study of the way the townspeople conceived of growth, health, and illness; and perhaps, in the manner of students of culture and personality, we would have had to give psychological tests to townspeople and to interpret their culture as a psychological projection of their inmost states of mind.

On the other hand, we learned some things about the world view of the townspeople which we have not included in the present study because they occupied a peripheral rather than a central place in their world view. For the most part these things had to do with nature, that part of the world which is non-human and non-supernatural. They were either items of empirical knowledge about plants and animals, the seasons and the land, or fragments of folklore. By claiming that they were on the periphery of the world view of the townspeople we do not mean that they lacked all significance, but only that Mitleños were more concerned with comprehending and regulating their social relationships, and with questions about the reality, efficacy and moral significance of supernatural beings; and, so far as we know, they had no general conceptions of the shape and order of the universe at large which brought their conceptions of nature into any definite and remarkable relation with their conceptions of human relations and the supernatural.

What we have done in the following chapters is to choose for analysis segments of the Mitleño outlook which determined the *general* character of that outlook and which were close to the level of self-awareness of townspeople. We have written about the things that our friends and acquaintances told us in words and unmistakable gestures were the more meaningful things in their lives. The result, which we did not anticipate until we had nearly completed the present manuscript, is that a single theme, now in the foreground, now in the background, runs through our account: the conception townspeople had of what it meant to be civilized.

In developing our understanding of the Mitleño world view it goes without saying that we have benefited from ideas developed by many outstanding anthropologists, but we have also found indispensable certain ideas elaborated by men in disciplines other than anthropology. Lionel Trilling, the literary critic; Samuel Taylor Coleridge, the poet; Reed Whittemore, the satirist; Henri Bergson, the philosopher; R. H. Tawney and Johan Huizinga, the historians—all have provided us with concepts which have tied together and illuminated the social and human meaning of our ethnographic observations.

Almost the entire state of Oaxaca is mountainous, but in the center of the state three long, narrow valleys radiate from the hub of the capital city, also called Oaxaca. These mild valleys with their provincial state capital and abundant Precolumbian ruins are a pride of Mexico. At the far end of the valley that runs east from the capital, and connected with the capital by a twenty-mile stretch of the Pan-American Highway, is the Zapotec-speaking town of Mitla, which is the subject of our study.

The 1950 national census counted 215,651 Zapotec-speaking people in the state of Oaxaca. In that census, Zapotec was listed as a single language. There are, however, six Zapotec languages. They are about as different from each other as are the Romance languages: French, Spanish, Italian, etc. Three different Zapotec languages are spoken in the mountains north and east of the city of Oaxaca, and two others are spoken respectively in the mountains south of the capital and in the Isthmus of Tehuantepec. The townspeople of Mitla speak the Zapotec language of the central valleys, but, as in several other Zapotec languages, there are distinct local dialects in different towns.[3]

Nearly one fourth of the Indian-speaking population of Mexico lives in Oaxaca. In the whole state, the 1950 census counted 583,853 people speaking sixteen different Indian languages, and we have just seen that further subdivisions of languages could have been listed. This great linguistic diversity, combined with the mountainous terrain which gives rise to a variety of ecological zones and many degrees of isolation of communities from the national society, presents to the anthropologist an exceedingly interesting area for study.

In Mitla my wife and I wrote field notes and shared our experiences of learning about the town. For the most part I have used the pronoun "we" in the body of this work not in the editorial sense, but to refer to both of us. We rented from a townsperson a house that was located in a neighborhood away from the center of town. By the standards of the community it was an ordinary house: neither large nor small, it had a dirt floor and an altar similar to those of most townspeople. The yard was relatively open to the street and to the yards of our neighbors. We visited daily with neighbors, and our son ranged wherever he could find playmates. Almost continuously during the year, there were ceremonies somewhere in Mitla, and we attended them even when we were not invited. We were always welcomed, and gained friends and acquaintances throughout the community.

Most adults in Mitla spoke Spanish, and we learned to use only a few phrases of the Zapotec dialect of the town. At ceremonies people often voluntarily translated conversations for us, or switched the conversation to Spanish so that we could understand. Several of our neighbors preferred to talk Zapotec to us while another neighbor, the brother of our maid, acted as a voluntary interpreter. They understood Spanish, however, and occasionally interrupted his translations to make corrections.

Although we explained to townspeople that I was going to write a book about Mitla, we did not take notes during ceremonies or conversations. We wrote our field notes from memory, seldom going more than a day or two without spending several hours at the typewriter. However, visitors sometimes interrupted us at the typewriter, and occasionally some of our friends dictated folktales to us.

Since we wanted to study the world view of the community, itself a composite of the world views of all of the members of the community, we formed friendships with men and women who lived in all of the neighborhoods of Mitla, who followed a variety of occupations and possessed other contrasting social and personal characteristics. Different townspeople looked at their community and their own lives within it from different points of view. In a common-sense way, we have taken these differences into account in our research.

During the last four months of our stay in Mitla I wrote a long description of the world view of townspeople. I occasionally translated parts of the manuscript to visitors in order to ask their opinion of it. I used real names in that manuscript, as did Elsie Clews Parsons in an earlier ethnographic study of Mitla.[4] Townspeople enjoyed looking at Parsons' book, identifying familiar names and the pictures of themselves or their friends. For this reason we have used the names of townspeople in the present work, with one exception where we have used false initials because the events discussed involve dangerous criminal behavior.

Our analysis of the world view of Mitleños begins in Chapter II. In Chapter I we summarize the recent history of Mitla, our reason being that throughout this study we describe the world view of townspeople as it has evolved under the pressure of social change. By analyzing the nature of the community during the past twenty years, and by reasoning from our knowledge of the region as a whole, we outline changes in the life of the community which have resulted in large part from an expansion of commerce in Oaxaca. This commercial expansion began in the latter part of the nineteenth century and continues to the present time. The reader who wishes to do so may begin with Chapter II and read only what we have written about the world view of townspeople in that and the subsequent chapters of this work.

Contents

Illustrations

I. Social Change in the Community and the Region

Between 1929 and 1933 Elsie Clews Parsons made three ethnological field trips to Mitla, and her book, *Mitla, Town of the Souls*, was published in 1936. My wife and four-year-old son and I lived in Mitla from May 1953, to May 1954. We selected a town whose general ethnography had already been recorded so that we could devote all of our time to learning the point of view of the townspeople.

Parsons' book, written in the comprehensive tradition of folkloristic ethnology, contains a prodigious number of ethnographic observations assembled in omnibus chapters with such titles as "Economic Life," "Lore and Tales," "Government," and "Religion." It does not possess any well-defined theoretical orientation, but, reflecting its author's wide experience, patience and sympathy for village life, it is one of our most intimate records of life in a Mesoamerican community.

Parsons stated the aim of her study in these terms:

> . . . My task is to convey the insight which I got among the Zapoteca into the ways in which the traits of an old culture may perish or survive, and the traits of a new culture come to be adopted or rejected. For the most part, the analysis is concerned with acculturation, with what the Indian culture took from the Spanish rather than with assimilation, which is a reciprocal process and would include consideration of what the early Spaniard took from the Indian in the development of both Spaniard and Indian into the modern Mexican.[1]

Her conception of the study of acculturation required that she find "touchstones by which to learn what is Spanish, what Indian." But by the time she studied Mitla she had formed a generalized image of Indian culture from her field work with the Pueblo Indians of the United States, from modern ethnological literature, and from the reports of colonial writers. This image was evidently the touchstone she used in assessing Mitla. There is no evidence in her book that she derived or modified her touchstone by observing communities in Oaxaca.

In looking for things related to her conception of Indian culture Parsons saw and described Mitleño traits which another observer might have missed altogether.

> I noted the low, self-contained voices, Indian voices, the unhurried gait of the barefoot women with bowl or basket on their head, their small hands and feet, the quiet children playing adult, the composure of all the townspeople, their order and style, and sentimentally I felt at home; the people reminded me of my Pueblo friends; the very town with its trickling river and mesalike boundaries recalled the town of the Ashiwi, Zuni, the most endearing of all our southwestern pueblos.[2]

Despite the clear-cut statement of her aim, Parsons' published study overflowed into an almost miscellaneous collection of ethnographic observations. At times, indeed, her book reads like a diary. One chapter, almost a hundred pages long, is composed exclusively of excerpts from her field notes. But we might better compare this aspect of her book to a loving and exuberant album of snapshots, and call it her photographic study of Mitla. Within its limits, a photograph is a superior document for determining what was actually before the camera. Throughout the present study we have related our observations to Parsons' photographs. We have neglected what seems to us the somewhat eccentric interpretation she brought to her materials through an overriding interest in cultural traits which may have originated in Precolumbian times.

We went to Mitla in 1953 to study something we called world view, not to study social change. But because we wanted to relate our study to Parsons' description of Mitla as it was twenty years earlier, we inevitably asked questions about change. There were the most immediate questions: was Eligio Santiago still alive? and his mother? Were there still the same number of town officials? Was the custom still practiced of burying an adult with a small bag containing articles for his soul to use on its journey? Such questions occupied us throughout the year. The answers we received revealed that Mitla had not changed greatly during the interval between Parsons' study and our own.

But, working from what we have called the photographic aspect of Parsons' report, we will describe the changes we did find in the community, and then show how these changes were related to more comprehensive changes in the region. By locating Parsons' study and ours in a regional context we will be able to give a general account of the recent history of Mitla that will prepare the way for subsequent chapters on the world view of townspeople.

Indian Communities in Mesoamerica

If one reads Parsons' monograph and then turns to the article by Professors Robert Redfield and Sol Tax, "General Characteristics of Present-Day Mesoamerican Indian Society," one realizes the close resemblance between Mitla and numerous other towns in Mesoamerica. Food and clothing and housing are much alike throughout the area, and numerous customs associated with birth, marriage, illness, death and other recurrent events are widely distributed. Social groupings and the ordering of social activities in general follow a common pattern. Let us review this pattern before recounting the particulars of Mitleño institutions. Our purpose in doing so is to designate the type of community to which Mitla belonged at the time of both Parsons' study and our own.

Although the typical Mesoamerican community is related to larger social entities through numerous national and regional institutions, such as governmental offices, markets in which money is the standard of exchange, and patterns of religious pilgrimage, the townspeople cultivate an intense identification with their local group. Most mar-

3

riages are contracted within the community, and individuals who live in a town other than the one to which their immediate family is felt traditionally to belong are considered to be outsiders.

The solidarity of the community is symbolized by the church and the image of the patron saint, by the edifice which houses the civil government, and by the interconnected hierarchies of civil and religious offices through which adult men periodically assume responsibility in the conduct of community affairs. Among those who speak the Indian language of the community there are great differences in status based on differences in wealth and personal achievements, but these status differences are not organized along class lines and are considerably less intense than those which separate townspeople who speak the Indian dialect from all others. The language of the town is, therefore, another outstanding symbol of local solidarity.

In Mitla there are no formal social groupings intermediate between the family and the local community. In this respect the town differs from many Mesoamerican Indian towns, in which some sort of territorial subdivisions exist. The family groups in Mitla are similar to those in the typical Mesoamerican town in that households are ordinarily composed of conjugal families, and occasionally cooperative multiple households are formed by closely related families occupying adjoining dwellings. In addition, the web of kinship is reinforced and extended through the frequently used Catholic institution of godparenthood, which provides a way of ritually dignifying relationships with other families.

The primary rhythm of social activity within the community is generated by an annual cycle of agricultural activities and religious festivals. The celebrations for the patron saint of the town, for Easter, and for All Souls' are the most important, and sometime during his career every man, assisted by his family and friends, is expected to undertake the responsibility of financing and organizing one or more festivals for the community-owned images of saints.

Besides these patterns of conduct, Mitla exhibits many others outlined by Redfield and Tax as typical of Mesoamerican Indian communities.

Having suggested Mitla's basic character, let us review Parsons' specific description of the town between 1929 and 1933, after which we can consider the changes which have occurred since that time.

Mitla, 1929–1933

One of the most striking characteristics of the townspeople revealed by Parsons' report was their interest in the market. Mitleños resembled the Maya-speaking Indians of the Guatemalan highlands as Sol Tax describes them. "The Indian," he writes, "is perhaps above all else an entrepreneur, a business man, always looking for new means of turning a penny."[3] Parsons was amazed by the pecuniary habits of Mitleños, and recorded several incidents such as the following:

> I remark on the black corn ears hanging in a circlet above the altar. In this household where more *creencias,* beliefs, linger on than in any other household I know, perhaps I can learn something of interest about the use of black corn. "The dark ears are very cheap," says Ligul, starting to take one down to give me. "They sell at 12 centavos. *Gente de razón* will eat only the white. We eat the yellow and the dark ones."

To which Parsons added, "Price, price, price! Instead of a ritual, a price list! A ritual of price!"[4] Of her main informant and interpreter she observed, "In Eligio's conception of modernism freedom to become a capitalist bulks large."[5] Like many of his townsmen Eligio was a trader. These men sold manufactured goods in isolated mountain towns where they bought coffee for resale in the valley. They were financed by wealthy Mitleño merchants who bought their coffee, and some of them, like Eligio, hoped eventually to accumulate enough capital to become merchants themselves.

But not only traders and merchants were involved in commerce. The household was rare in which some members of the family were not occasionally engaged in buying goods for resale. People would buy a small supply of goods to sell in their homes, or in the plaza market, or at regional fairs, or at the ruins, where tourists came.

5

In contrast to commerce, farming was an occupation with little appeal to townspeople. The land around Mitla was arid and unproductive. Agriculture as a way of life was associated with poverty and drudgery.[6] Occupational possibilities were multifarious in a town the size of Mitla —there were leather working, carpentry, masonry, baking, barbering, weaving, distilling, well-digging, domestic service, curing. But the most exciting and by far the most profitable occupation was commerce. The fascination of townspeople with buying and selling led Parsons to conclude, "Today the inroads of change are not through the Church, but through capitalism."[7]

As in any community in which the pursuit of gain in the market place is a favored occupation, prestige differences corresponded closely to differences in wealth. However, there lived in Mitla a few large landowners and descendants of such owners who were "outstanding personalities in the life of the town," and formed "the nucleus of that class which I began by saying does not exist—*los correctos.*" They were not, and probably did not want to be, full members of the community, and, according to Parsons, they did not form a distinct social class but were "merely individuals possessed of more or less influence which will take form as class influence in a few decades or even years . . . when *idioma* will be spoken only in the fringes of the town, its Indian fringes, *el Centro* having become the center of the 'right people.' "[8]

The influence of these people on the life of the town depended not only on the wealth they derived from their landholdings, but also on their position as intermediaries between townspeople and national institutions. By the time of Parsons' field work, however, changes wrought throughout the nation by the Mexican Revolution had reduced their political and economic hold on the community, and the Zapotec-speaking merchants who were engaged in the coffee trade had approached or surpassed them in wealth and prestige.

Parsons did not analyze the status differences and system of social ranking in Mitla, but, whether or not we agree with her assertion that there were no social classes, her report contains ample evidence that (1) differences in occupation, literacy and many other attributes, besides wealth, were responsible for considerable differences in rank and status within the community; (2) Mitleños ordinarily thought of their town as socially heterogeneous; and (3) they habitually used two sets of categories to characterize people: "the rich and the poor," and "the city person and the Indian."

The social identification based on speaking the Zapotec dialect of the town was particularly valued by the townspeople, but within the language community the dominant motives of economic practice and of status differentiation were divisive: to gain personal advantage in a competitive market and to institutionalize social discriminations. By comparison, the political and religious institutions of the community contributed more overtly to the intense sentiment of local solidarity. The outlines of these institutions were partially defined by the system of town service which was called simply *servicio.*

There were about fifty town offices to be filled each year. The town council was elected, but all other officials were appointed. The incumbents of offices held by appointment nominated their successors, with the council making the appointments by approving such nominations. The council was composed of five men, including the president and the superintendent of public works, and five substitutes, one of whom was the substitute president and one the substitute superintendent. These were the town offices of greatest prestige, with the president in the highest position, the superintendent the next in rank, and the rest of the council of equal prestige. Offices held by appointment also differed in prestige. The highest ranking positions were those of the justices of the peace and their substitutes. Among the lowest were those whose incumbents acted as policemen and as errand boys for the council.

All male citizens were expected to hold a series of offices, beginning low in the hierarchy and moving up. Eligibility for election to the town council or for appointment as a justice of the peace was earned by serving in lower offices, and by acting as the sponsor for a saint's celebration (*mayordomía*). Each man was expected to sponsor two *mayordomías* during his life. For a single year Parsons listed twenty-one *mayordomías.*

The offices of *fiscales,* which carried the duty of supervising community-wide religious festivals, were traditionally occupied by men in their final year of town service. And yet these men were inferior in prestige

7

to members of the council and to justices of the peace. And men who had completed their years of service had no special authority or influence in the conduct of civic affairs. They merely gained the personal respect due to elders who had lived a life consistent with social expectations.

The system of town service did not provide a government without sharp political controversies. Such controversies were accompanied, however, by public expressions of political unity and peacefulness. Thus, townspeople asserted that their political solidarity was both fact and ideal.

While most political activity and an important sector of religious endeavor were encompassed by the system of town service, a large part of the religious life of the community was outside its bounds. Weddings and funerals, for example, provided occasions for prolonged and elaborate ceremonials which had no relation to *servicio*. For one interested in the general character of the community, an important aspect of these ceremonials, and of *mayordomías*, too, was the manner in which they were financed. The expense of funerals was borne directly by the family and godparents, aided by voluntary contributions from close friends, but weddings and *mayordomías* were financed through a system of reciprocal loans called *guelagueza*. Those who were invited to a wedding or to a saint's celebration were expected to contribute substantial amounts of money, food, or other goods. Each guest's contribution was carefully recorded and had to be returned in kind when he undertook a similar festival. Considering the large number and size of such ceremonials, the resulting network of debts and credits formed a most important part of the social fabric. Further, these exchanges, conducted in the manner of gift-giving, were resonant with ethical and sentimental meanings which increased feelings of communal solidarity.

Mitla, 1953–1954

In the twenty years between Parsons' study and our own, most Mitleños stopped wearing white trousers and shirts and adopted styles of clothing more closely resembling those of working-class city people.

8

New styles of music gained popularity in the community and several men bought marimbas. The ritual candles for *mayordomías,* and the cross of quicklime used in funerals acquired new and more elaborate decorations.

The *haciendas* were expropriated, their lands distributed among those who cultivated them. A paved highway was built which connected Mitla to the state capital and the world beyond. A post office was opened, and a tax collector's office. A Mexican doctor established residence in Mitla. A retired businessman from Minneapolis bought one of the big houses on the plaza, and Protestant missionaries from the United States settled in town.

These events and numerous others constitute the recent history of Mitla. But they have not resulted in any radical change in the manners of its inhabitants, still less in their social structure. We mean by manners what Lionel Trilling calls the "hum and buzz of implication . . . the whole evanescent context" of the culture of the community.[9] As Trilling has said, any complex culture exhibits not one system of manners but a conflicting variety of such systems. This is certainly true of Mitla as Parsons reported it and as we observed it, and much of the material in subsequent chapters centers on the various implications of conflicting manners in Mitla. But the immediate question is whether a decided change had occurred in the manners of townspeople during the twenty years previous to our study, to which our answer is no. The evidence for this assertion will be found in later chapters where we relate our observations of Mitleño manners to Parsons' report.

The expropriation of the *haciendas,* the opening of a paved highway, etc., are striking events which suggest the possibility that profound changes have taken place in the social structure of Mitla. Raymond Firth nicely defined such changes as consisting of "those social relations which seem to be of critical importance for the behaviour of members of the society, so that if such relations were not in operation, the society could not be said to exist in that form."[10] When we compare our observations with those reported by Parsons, however, we cannot say that Mitla has become a different kind of community, that social rela-

9

tions have changed in such a way and to such a degree that the form of communal life is different.

The first expropriation of one of the two *haciendas* of Mitla was completed in 1934, less than a year after Parsons' last visit to Mitla, and the expropriation of the second, shortly thereafter. But these actions were only the denouement of the decline from power in town affairs of the *hacendados*. Few townsmen benefited from the redistribution of land, which went to Spanish-speaking peasants who lived in small settlements on the *haciendas*. The highway, the new governmental offices, the Mexican doctor, and the resident North Americans brought the outside world closer to the community of Zapotec-speaking townspeople, but they maintained a relationship to that world not unlike the one that Parsons described. Status distinctions within the community were still considerably less sharp than those which separated Mitleños from outsiders. Nor were townspeople divided by organized political factions. Commerce remained the most fascinating occupation to townspeople, and they still specialized in trade between the mountain towns and the valley markets. The hierarchy of political offices and the *mayordomía* were still the institutions through which the system of town service was organized. Such changes as had occurred were within-system changes. Minor offices had been added to the political hierarchy, a few offices had been dropped, and the *mayordomías* were more numerous than in 1929–33.

Are we to conclude that Mitla was a static society? We do not think so. We must conclude rather that the interval between Parsons' study and ours simply did not comprehend a segment of history which revealed the dynamics of social change in Mitla. For such revelation we must begin with Mitla in the nineteenth century.

Mitla from the Late Nineteenth Century to the Present

Mitleños themselves were aware of important changes in their community. They expressed this awareness by saying, "Now we are civilized," and they identified civilization with a number of characteristics

10

of their community. In a later chapter we will analyze their conceptions of Mitla as a peaceful, civilized, politically unified community in which outsiders were welcome to live and work. But the most obvious proofs of civilization to townspeople were the myriad indications of their involvement with urban, industrial centers—the many bright advertisements for beer and cigarettes and soft drinks, the numerous stores with shelves of manufactured goods, the coming and going of trucks and buses. Commerce, and the visible consequences of commerce, gave life an excitement upon which the townspeople throve.

According to Julio de la Fuente, the commercial cultivation of coffee in the mountains north of Mitla began in the late nineteenth century and developed rapidly.[11] By the end of the century a number of merchants in Yalalag, a Zapotec-speaking town in the mountains, had become wealthy by exploiting the commercial naivete of the rustic coffee growers. Mitleños, already accustomed to making trading journeys, began to do the same thing. And at this time the central valleys of Oaxaca were joined to the outside world by a railroad; subsequently transportation to and from national and even international markets became steadily cheaper and faster.

Throughout the state of Oaxaca towns specialized in producing a variety of foods and craft products for the regional market. Before the improvements in transportation and communication and the development of cash crops in the isolated mountain villages, this regional market system was largely independent of national and international markets. Economic relations with extra-regional institutions were almost exclusively the concern of a small group whose wealth was derived from political office, from a small gold mining industry, or, most important, from the ownership of large estates in those productive agricultural lands with access to the capital city. Thus, a dual market system prevailed, with production and exchange in the regional market, which was the dominant interest of the bulk of the population, remaining quite distinct from the national and international markets. Rustic villagers had little use for money. Even today Mitleño traders have difficulty using paper money in the mountains, where villagers, unable to read, often cannot distinguish one note from another. Instead, traders deal almost exclusively with coins, whose value villagers recognize by their size and weight.

As the regional market merged with national and international markets, the basis of wealth and power shifted from land ownership to commerce. The Mexican Revolution then achieved a large-scale reorientation of national institutions, which officially sanctioned economic as well as political democracy.

Since Mitla was in the mainstream of the expansion of commerce in Oaxaca, one might expect that it would suffer from social disintegration under the impact of the outside world. While this is true, much of our analysis of the Mitleño world view in subsequent chapters will demonstrate that conflicting expectations, incompatible ideals, and disparities between ideals and practice were not only lived with but were sometimes skillfully transformed and reconciled by complex stylistic elements in the culture of the community. Furthermore, the prosperity of Mitla, stemming from its role as a community of merchants and traders in a period of rapid commercial expansion, contributed to its success in maintaining a greater degree of social integration than has been maintained in other, less prosperous towns in the region. The most obvious connection between Mitla's prosperity and its resistance to disintegration resides in the fact that the townspeople turned a significant part of their increased wealth into expenditures on *mayordomías* and other ceremonials. Whether this public spirit would have persisted if still more opportunities had existed for the profitable investment of savings is a question which must await further research into the history of the town. But in the recent past, townspeople have spent a large part of their income on festivals that contributed to sentiments of social well-being and solidarity.

If we assume that *mayordomías* were one significant index of the relative integration of communities in this area of Oaxaca, it is interesting to compare Mitla's record in respect to them with that of neighboring towns.[12] In 1953–54, Mitla honored twenty-four saints with *mayordomías*. Teotitlán del Valle, which was about the same size as Mitla and in appearance approximately as well off, had fifteen *mayordomías*. But other nearby towns, obviously less prosperous, had only two or three. In these towns the practice had been abandoned of requiring a man to sponsor a saint's festival to become eligible for holding important political offices. These communities were occasionally torn by violent political factionalism. The newspaper in the capital often reported such disputes, and every so often the state government dispatched troops to restore order. In addition, several of these towns were depopulating. So many houses had been abandoned in one community near Mitla that it had taken on the aspect of a ghost town. The population of Mitla, on the other hand, had slowly but steadily increased: the 1921 census showed 2,007 residents. Ten years later Parsons estimated the population to be 2,500.[13] A census taken in 1949 showed 2,690; another in 1953 counted 2,951.[14]

To recapitulate, the major change which had occurred in Mitla since the end of the nineteenth century consisted in its transition from a society in which power and wealth were based on the ownership of large landed estates to a society in which power and wealth were based on commerce. In a recent study of the market at Tlaxiaco, a town in the Upper Mixteca sub-region of Oaxaca, Alejandro Marroquín describes this change in the following words:

> The agrarian reforms of the Revolution shattered the socio-economic equilibrium of the villages; the *hacienda,* center of gravity of the former system, disappeared and the natives searched anxiously for a new principle to restore order and stability to the resulting social upheaval; the store of the important merchant became the new center of gravity of the region, with the merchant in his patriarchal role substituting for the *hacendado;* the great merchant, both exploiting and aiding the production of the natives, presents himself to them as a generous provider of charity and favors.[15]

Our contention, however, is that in Mitla this transition had begun well before the Revolution, that the Revolution merely confirmed and accelerated a trend which was already well developed. We would summarize the history of this transition in Mitla in some such terms as these: Beginning in the last decades of the nineteenth century, a growing number of Mitleños acquired wealth through commerce, and this wealth created an increasing demand for special services of all kinds. Thus, an individual's status was determined more and more by individual achievement, less and less by the possession of land or even by the system of town service. By 1929–33, for instance, men did not receive any special recognition for having completed their town service, and the offices of *fiscales,* traditionally occupied by men in their final year of *servicio,* were not of high rank. Money competed with sacred rituals and kinship in defining social relationships and produced what Parsons aptly called a ritual of price. But much of the increasing income of the townspeople was used to enlarge the traditional festivals of the community. In this manner changing status relationships were both accommodated and "socialized," and Zapotec-speaking merchants replaced the *hacendados* as the persons with greatest authority in local affairs.

II. History and Myth

... Every historical change creates its mythology.
—Bronislaw Malinowski [1]

Did Mitleños create a mythology in response to the transformation of their lives brought about by the expansion of commerce in Oaxaca? When in the nineteenth century our own society underwent great commercial changes, we developed a mythology of the self-made man whose aggressively selfish behavior won moral approbation as well as fame and fortune. In Mitla quite another evaluation was often made of economic success. Stories were told that wealthy individuals had sold themselves to the devil. The notion was that these people, either through accidental encounters with the devil or by visiting caves where the devil could always be petitioned, contracted to exchange their souls for wealth. And, when the devil came to take them away, they tried to prolong their enjoyment of this world by persuading him to take one of their employees instead.[2]

Most of the Mitleños we knew discounted some of these stories as envious gossip, but they told others with expressions of complete conviction. The successful merchants in Mitla openly ridiculed devil contract stories, saying that the people who told them were motivated by envy, ignorance and superstition. They disclaimed any belief at all in devils. And, despite the fact that these stories were frequently told, most people did not modify their behavior in any apparent way because of them. They did not, for instance, avoid association with the

15

individuals about whom they told such stories. But the conduct of a few townspeople was directly guided by the lore of devil contract stories. One of our neighbors quit his job for fear that his wealthy employer planned to turn him over to the devil, and the two caves near town which were reputed to be places where individuals could petition the devil were in fact visited by some townspeople who hoped thereby to gain wealth.[3]

Most townspeople fell between the extremes of those who forcefully debunked devil contract stories and those who firmly believed them. They talked and acted as if there was, however remote, some possibility that one could gain wealth from transactions with the devil. Although they recognized the distorting motives of jealousy and anger that prompted people to gossip about the devil-who-gave-wealth,[4] they found in these stories a way of criticizing the almost universal practice of sharp dealing in economic affairs. Since townspeople also assumed that such behavior was the necessary price of success in the intensely competitive economy of the region (see Chapter VII, "The Acquisitive Society"), they were prone to believe that individuals who gained extraordinary wealth went farther than others in violating community ideals of spontaneous honesty and generosity.

Although the devil contract stories were told as true accounts of recent events, they were not historical in the sense of expressing an awareness of social change. On the contrary, townspeople said that the same tales circulated in the past about the Spanish-speaking landowners. These stories cannot, therefore, be taken as illustrative of the way historical changes lead to the creation of a new mythology. Rather they extended an already existing myth to a different but similarly placed category of people.

Emergent Images of a New Mythology

No single myth dramatized the social transformation that had occurred in Mitla during the preceding fifty years, but the beginnings of such a myth were discernible in the accounts of the man who domi-

Neighbors, members of one of the wealthier families in Mitla.

Pedro Santiago, his wife, daughters, and grandnephew.

A Mitla bride and groom seated between the groom's parents, with the marriage go-between and a family elder standing.

nated the town about a generation ago.[5] Don Félix owned the only store in town and lived in the biggest house on the plaza. He was said to have owned a great deal of land which he obtained when townspeople pawned their property to him. Any townsman who went into his store had to remove his hat and cross his arms over his chest as a gesture of respect while he waited to be recognized. Then Don Félix in his own good time would address him in a gruff and condescending manner.

The accounts of Don Félix and his family which circulated in Mitla represented a community of humble, poor and easily exploited townspeople who knew little of the world outside the boundaries of their village lands. This representation contrasted with the conception of contemporary Mitla as a commercially oriented community of urbane townspeople capable of asserting and protecting their interests. The phrase, "Now we are civilized," perfectly expressed for townspeople this newer community image.

Insofar as we think of myth as having qualities of fiction, it is significant that Don Félix was in fact dead before some of the events took place in which he was said to have participated. One of these events was related to us several times to exemplify his cruelty and humiliation when his orphan niece bore the child of an Indian servant. The girl refused to tell Don Félix the name of her lover. Infuriated, he beat her and locked her in the barn. There, unaided by a midwife, she delivered her baby in the manger!

Sometime after the death of Don Félix, his son-in-law attempted to take his place in the community. This young man, Don Rafael, tried to become the president of Mitla in the early 1930's, but by this time several Zapotec-speaking coffee merchants had risen to wealth and prominence, and Don Rafael was rejected in a political argument serious enough to bring authorities from the state capital to make a settlement.[6] Ten years later he succeeded in becoming president, and the story of one of the events that followed was told us several times with an excitement and satisfaction which indicated that more than the event itself was involved.

17

There was a traditional curfew in the period immediately preceding the festival for Mitla's patron saint. Anyone found on the streets by the town police late at night was arrested and fined as a way of raising money and recruiting labor for the expenses of the celebration. Don Rafael supposedly decided to mark his period of office by an unusually large festival and so he personally led the police in enforcing the curfew with tyrannical severity. The situation was intolerable until the son-in-law of a highly successful merchant hid a pistol under his shirt and late one night stood at a street corner near the center of town playing his guitar and singing.

Don Rafael tried to arrest this young man, but his police deserted him and he was unable to get any of the other officials of the town to give him support. Besides being pleased to see someone defy Don Rafael, they were afraid to antagonize the culprit. Don Rafael ranted and shot his pistols into the air, but when he had exhausted his ammunition his adversary gave him a sound thrashing. "After this," concluded a friend of ours, "no one had any respect for Don Rafael." This statement was weighted with meaning, for Mitleños considered the ability to command respect to be a fundamental condition for entering into social relationships. A person who was not respected was constantly exposed to insults, and even to the danger of physical injury.

We did not discover how much of this story was historically true. We suggest, however, that its popularity and the emotional satisfaction with which it was told indicate that it had acquired qualities which are usually attributed to myths. The several times we heard the story it was related by people who were not themselves witnesses to any of the events, despite which they told it at length and with careful attention to detail. Furthermore, an internal analysis of the story strongly suggests that its significance resided, at least in part, in the fact that it dramatized the primary social change which had occurred in Mitla in recent times. Let us make such an analysis.

Don Rafael was portrayed as an old-time exploiter dressed in the dark clothing of the city and wearing pistols prominently displayed in holsters. He spoke only Spanish and had aggressive manners. Finally, he was not a native member of the community, but had moved to Mitla when he married into the family of Don Félix.

In contrast, the young man who challenged Don Rafael conformed to a popular image of the new Mitla. He was not himself wealthy, but his father-in-law was said to be the richest merchant in town. He was born in Mitla, and both he and his father-in-law spoke Zapotec, wore sandals, and shared many other characteristics which associated him with the new class of traders. He carried a pistol in order to resist intimidation, but it was hidden under his clothing lest he give offense by *appearing* aggressive. And, in playing a guitar and singing in the street, he borrowed one of the city customs admired by townspeople. Most of all, his willingness to assert himself against the exploitive use of the curfew brought utter humiliation to a foreign tyrant and vindicated local autonomy and dignity.

A dominating idea in Mitleño political ideology was that Mitla was a peaceful community. Mitleños viewed the continuous squabbling and occasional violence in their town as the consequence of *individual* disagreements. The important thing was that there were no organized social factions. Physical combat provides potent dramatic material for symbolizing transition, however, and the story of Don Rafael's humiliation by a son of the town was consistent with the image of a peaceful and united community since it appeared to describe no more than a conflict between individuals. At the same time it dramatized the great events of the last fifty years and the emergence of the new Mitleño—independent, self-reliant, sophisticated—the hero of a "civilized" town.

Myth and the Imagination

Malinowski observed that myth-making is "an explicit development into narrative of certain crucial points in native belief." [7] But what happens to myth-making in a community where the belief system itself is changing? Malinowski did not deal with this situation in the Trobriand Islands, nor did E. R. Leach, whose analysis of Kachin social structure in highland Burma is perhaps the most significant contribution to the sociological theory of myth in recent years.[8]

In his attempt to penetrate the confusions of a fluctuating social structure, Leach analyzed the uses of myth and ritual in the political polemics of a culturally and socially heterogeneous region where communities oscillated between feudalistic and primitive democratic political forms. He concluded that *all* actual social systems are in disequilibrium, but that anthropologists can only analyze them by reference to fictional models of societies in equilibrium. He then showed that in the Kachin hills people understood the contradictions in their society and, as partisans on one side or the other, attempted to manipulate their fellows by using rhetorical appeals based on fictions similar to the models of the anthropologists.

Leach asserted that Malinowski and a number of other leading social anthropologists had confused their "equilibrium models" with reality, one result of which had been a misapprehension in their work of the essential nature of myth and ritual.

Myth and ritual is a language of signs in terms of which claims to rights and status are expressed but it is a language of argument, not a chorus of harmony. If ritual is sometimes a mechanism of integration, one could as well argue that it is often a mechanism of disintegration.[9]

In his analysis of political factionalism, however, Leach treated the conceptions of a lineage-based equalitarian (*gumsa*) society and a hierarchical patronage (*gumlao*) society as if they were part of an unchanging dialectic of political ideals. He did not ignore history, but he viewed the history of the Kachin region as a series of intrusions by outside powers (Chinese, Burmese, and British) and of reactions to these intrusions in which one or the other pole of the *gumsa-gumlao* dialectic was strengthened.

In Mitla the story of the young man's battle with Don Rafael was obviously part of a polemic in which two different forms of society were seen in opposition, with the young man's victory serving as propaganda for one of them. This story, then, fits Leach's conception of the function of myth. But other stories current in Mitla reveal processes of cultural change which Leach neglected. Before describing these stories it will be useful to review Samuel Taylor Coleridge's distinction between Imagination and Fancy, for it is a distinction which will add to our understanding of what happens to myths when a society experiences a fundamental cultural change.

"The Imagination," Coleridge tells us, "modifies images, and gives unity to variety; it sees all things in one." The Fancy, on the other hand, presents "images which have no connection natural or moral." [10] Such images, having lost whatever profound relationship they may once have had to a culture, do not sum up a people's experience.

The Abe Lincoln log cabin myth, for example, was an expression of the imagination when it summed up the diverse experiences of nineteenth-century Americans, many of whom had in common an awareness of frontier conditions in which men could hope to mold their individual destinies free from the restraints of urban centers. But in the twentieth century the imagery of this myth has shifted into the realm of romantic fiction where, to use Coleridge's language, it is fanciful rather than imaginative and its power to command a moral and intellectual response is greatly reduced.

Now for the Mitleño legend which illustrates Coleridge's distinction. According to local tradition Mitla was the center of the world of the dead.[11] This tradition recalled a time before the sun appeared, when stone was as light as corn stalks and as soft as soap. When "the ancient ones" of that period heard that the sun was going to rise, they built the monuments whose ruins occupy the countryside in and around Mitla. Although "the ancient ones" were small, they carved and carried the stones, and in the cruciform subterranean chambers of the monuments they made the crossroads where the souls of the dead were to meet in the afterlife. They were still working when the sun rose and Jesus Christ brought the true religion. Then stone hardened and became heavy, and "the ancient ones" went underground where they turned into idols. But two of their leaders, an old man (*Gol Gisa*) and his wife (*Zus Lai*) received permission to stay above ground, and they turned to boulders on the hillside near the site where the stones for the monuments were quarried.

Parsons published stories about *Gol Gisa* and *Zus Lai* which tell of magical flights, talking animals, and other extraordinary phenomena associated with the legend of Mitla as the crossroads of the dead.[12] But the careful reader of Parsons' materials will find many evidences that these stories were mere fancies. She had difficulty finding informants who were willing to expatiate on them,[13] and she heard many expressions of uncertainty on the part of townspeople about the customs associated with such "Indian" lore. Furthermore, she was told that rituals formerly performed at the ruins on behalf of the dead had been abandoned, and she recorded what seemed to her the careless or confused atmosphere which frequently accompanied funeral as well as other rituals.

Our own observations confirmed those of Parsons. Parts of the rituals of death and of All Souls', and some narratives generally known by townspeople still referred to the legend of the town of the souls; but these references, in both the rituals and the narratives, were casual and disconnected. In some respects, at least, formal education and more intense contact with the larger society had narrowed the range of events that Mitleños conceived to be possible so that many elements in the traditional accounts of the long-ago seemed to them to be highly improbable. They expressed their doubts in such equivocal phrases as "There are *some* people who believe . . ." or *"They* say. . ." or *"Who knows* if it is true?"* Even though these narratives attributed a grand supernatural character to the community few townspeople were interested in telling them or knew their details.

The story of Don Rafael's triumph was a myth, or the beginning of a myth, which dramatized the outstanding social change in Mitla in recent years. It confirms Leach's notion that myths are among the weapons with which the battles between rival social ideals are fought. But the decayed legend of Mitla as the town of the souls was, for the very reason that it had lost most of its drama, no less significant an index of cultural change. The legend's attenuated hold on the imagination of townspeople suggested a pervasive change in their whole conception of reality. As Reed Whittemore has put it, "Myth works on a sliding scale." In one period in the history of a culture it may be more effective than in another, and there are periods when "it can only go to that point beyond 'facts' where it still looks like 'facts.' " [14]

Rather than being vital revelations of reality, stories about the time in which Mitla became the center of the world of the dead were tales of an anomalous character which townspeople regarded as possibly genuine though nonetheless quaint accounts of the past. When our conversations turned to this subject a townsperson would occasionally shrug his shoulders and smile, saying, "These things happened so long ago, who can say if they are really true, but they are *pretty!*"

III. Civilized Peacefulness and Violence

. . . When ideals have sunk to the level of practice, the result is stagnation.

—Alfred North Whitehead [1]

When Mitleños declared, "Now we are civilized," they often had in mind the notion that their town was an open, peaceful community of people who cultivated an urbane way of life. But the facts of life in Mitla were frequently contrary to this conception of the community.

Although townspeople insisted that theirs was an open community, they scornfully characterized the people of neighboring communities as ignorant, suspicious and prone to violence. And when individuals from those towns moved to Mitla, townspeople did not accept them as full members of their community. Although townspeople maintained that Mitla was a peaceful community, they knew that every day angry individuals went to the town officials with grievances against each other, and that arguments not uncommonly led to violence or the threat of violence. In 1953–54, there was even a disagreement among the town officials which threatened the peace of the entire community.

Individual Affairs and Public Peace

As soon as we settled in Mitla we began to hear about arguments and fights. In several of the fights individuals were injured, and in one an innocent bystander was killed. At the same time, townspeople told us that we should feel safe to go anywhere at any time. In other towns, they said, people could not go from one neighborhood to another at night for fear of attack, and there were political factions which sometimes led to the murder of town officials. If we lived in one of those towns we would have to be cautious. But in Mitla all conflicts were *particular,* the personal affairs of individuals. To be sure, there were always some disputatious people who caused trouble—that was human nature, they reasoned—but, unlike people in other towns where there were social divisions, Mitleños were not characteristically this way. They said that in Mitla people only fought over sexual affairs or property or because they were drunk. The motives were private and, so far as the community as a whole was concerned, trivial.

This was the *public* reasoning of townspeople; it was what they told outsiders, and it was what they often told one another. Was it self-deception? Did townspeople believe what they said? There is no simple answer, but we shall begin one by observing that townspeople were practiced and self-conscious liars.

We were always being told by one Mitleño that something someone else had told us was a lie. As a matter of fact, it was not difficult to discuss lying with townspeople as one of the recognized customs of the community. Its rules were simple and could be formulated by many townspeople in a manner only slightly less systematic than the following codification.

First, there were the minor lies people constantly told just to be agreeable, or to preserve the privacy of their own thoughts and acts, as when they casually promised to meet someone with no intention of doing so, or when they denied having seen a person whom they had just visited. These lies were told in accordance with good manners and common sense. When they misled people, or frustrated their curiosity, they were amusing; for the most part, however, they were conventions that no one expected anyone else to believe and that it would have been crude to challenge.

Then there were the gross lies, the ones people told when they attempted to take advantage of someone. Above all, such lies had to have

26

the semblance of truth, which required courage and boldness and an ability to invent falsehoods appropriate to the situation. Here the liar needed a lively discrimination of the personality and state of knowledge of the person to whom he was lying. Success in this kind of lying not only led to material reward, as when one gained money or sexual privileges, but also amused everyone except the person who was deceived.

About the only lies considered vicious and truly reprehensible were those whose purpose was to gull a close kinsman or friend. Unrelated people might laugh if such lies were ingenious, but their serious disapproval was never far off. This species of lying was a betrayal of *confianza,* and we will shortly see how important relationships of confidence were to townspeople.

Except where a breach of *confianza* was involved, Mitleños made lying into a comic art. Where the liar was successful, he demonstrated his cleverness and his superior judgment of people. When he failed, he exposed himself to ridicule for his ineptness, for his lack of boldness, or for his pettiness in seeking a trivial advantage through lying.

And yet the acceptance of lying as a custom of the community did not prevent the person wronged by a lie from feeling bitter, although it restrained him from seeking retaliation in such a way as to advertise his gullibility. Nor did it prevent townspeople generally from affirming in both acts and words their ideal of a really honest man. Liars that they were with those outside their intimate sphere of family and friends, townspeople strove to be truthful within this sphere, and they showed us in many small ways that they could be gratuitously honest with outsiders who gained their respect by respecting them.

Since townspeople commonly discounted each other's lies, it is interesting that no one ever told us that people lied when they claimed that Mitla was a peaceful, unified community in which incidents of violence were rare and insignificant. We must examine the ways in which townspeople interpreted a number of events which threatened the public peace in order to understand what their image of Mitla as a civilized community meant to them. Here is the way one Mitleño,

Pantaleón García, combined hyperbole and casuistry in his interpretation of specific episodes of violence.

Pantaleón began a conversation by praising the beauties of Mitla's landscape, the mildness of its climate, the gentleness of its citizens, and the charm of its festivals. How different all this was from other towns where there was constant fighting! Pantaleón had fresh evidence for this claim; only that day we had learned that two men were killed in a fight in Tlacolula, and recently the celebration for the patron saint of another neighboring town had been disrupted by fighting.

Having heard this sort of thing many times before, I decided to see how Pantaleón would react if I contested his claims by mentioning the fact that a number of Mitleños carried guns.

"Yes," Pantaleón responded, "but *under* their clothing, not outside."

"But when men carry guns they use them to kill," I protested.

"No, not in Mitla! Here when people shoot they shoot up into the air," Pantaleón said.

Recently a townsman, Margarito Santiago, had been killed by the stray pistol-shots of drunken brawlers. So I replied, "They didn't shoot into the air when they killed Margarito."

Pantaleón resorted to the conventional sentiment that Margarito's death was very sad but that every man had his time to die. He pointed his finger toward the ceiling: "It was God's decision."

Pedro Santiago, Margarito's father-in-law, was present during this conversation. He acquiesced in Pantaleón's interpretation, so I gently repeated what he had told me at his son-in-law's funeral, that Margarito died before his time, that he was killed without reason, that he was a man who worked hard to support his family and did not drink or roam the street.

"Very well," Pantaleón answered, "but the brawlers were just drunken boys, and it was not for divisions [social factions]."

Pedro Santiago, evidently not wishing to prolong what was for him an unpleasant conversation, agreed with both of us, and Pantaleón went on happily to the theme that fighting in Mitla was usually over women, and always *particular,* whereas in other towns. . . .

28

I asked Pantaleón if it was true, as I had heard, that the man who exhibited movies in Mitla came to town irregularly because he was afraid to follow a schedule since someone had shot at him the preceding spring from the bridge near the plaza.

"Yes, that's certain," he replied, going on to explain that this man had been on the governor's side the year before when the "revolution" occurred in the state which resulted in the governor's ouster. But this affair had nothing to do with Mitla because the exhibitor was from Tlacolula and so was the person who shot at him.

Thus amiably we discussed a murder, an attempted murder, and a recent "revolution"—none of them *really* concerns of the community as a whole.

Four months after the conversation with Pantaleón a man was murdered while working in the fields of his Mitleño employer. Although he was living and working in Mitla, townspeople said that he was not a member of their community. They explained that he was from Xaagá, and that the man who killed him was from Loma Larga. These are two Spanish-speaking settlements on the lands of the former *haciendas* in the *municipio* of Mitla.

The murdered man was said to have been himself a murderer who had only recently returned from taking refuge in the mountains. When his enemies heard that he was working in Mitla they ambushed him. To our acquaintances all of this simply proved how bad people in other communities were. So far as we could tell, it did not occur to them that the Mitleño employer should not have hired an alleged murderer to work for him, or that the man's death compromised their community's claim to peacefulness.

The case of R. J. provides another example of the way townspeople insisted that violence and the threat of violence were *particular*. R. J.'s wife was a Mitleña, but townspeople never neglected to emphasize that R. J. was from Tlacolula and consequently not one of them. His reputation among all of our acquaintances was that of a murderer who had moved to Mitla to escape being killed by the family of a man he had killed in his home town. The year before our stay in Mitla a townsman

29

had been stabbed to death, and this murder, too, was generally attributed to R. J. In addition, we were told that several years earlier a prominent Mitleño merchant hired R. J. and another man to kill a rival merchant, but R. J.'s would-be accomplice lost his nerve and informed the intended victim of the plot.

During our stay in Mitla, R. J. added to his crimes by stabbing a townsman in the back. L. A. told us about it soon after it happened. The stabbing occurred early in the morning on All Souls' Day. Stores were closed and the streets were deserted, and L. A. was visiting in a house near the center of town when he saw the wounded man staggering up the street from the river where he had been attacked only a few minutes earlier.

L. A. and his family were amazed when we asked who went out to help the man. They explained that someone hurried to his home to notify his family, and that a few minutes later his brother came for him. The picture L. A. drew of the situation was of people watching guardedly from their houses as the unaided man, howling and bleeding, tried to walk home. Despite our shocked protests, L. A. and his family considered this behavior to be simple common sense and morality. They explained that it was both bad and dangerous to interfere in the troubled affairs of other people, and they reaffirmed this wisdom when we proposed hypothetical cases. If one were to come upon the body of a murdered man, for instance, one should not say anything but wait for the town authorities to discover it. Or if men started fighting with deadly weapons one should run away, unless a number of people were present so that one could watch without being implicated.

An incident recorded by Parsons is especially worth quoting. "One night last summer in one of the streets of the town Manuel Quero was shot in the back from a shotgun and badly wounded. Probably by an irate husband, gossip goes, because Manuel is known to visit married women." One day Parsons went to visit Manuel Quero but his daughter told her that he had gone to his fields. That evening another person told her that the daughter had lied. "He is in town, in hiding, at the house of a *compadre*. They say it was he who shot at Manuel, the tailor, as he was returning from Tlacolula, eight days ago. Two men shot at him from a ditch on the road, ten shots, and they only wounded his horse. . . . Manuel Quero thought it was Manuel the tailor who shot him last summer."

"How long will Manuel Quero stay in hiding? Don't the *topiles* know where he is?" Parsons asked, and the answer was, "Yes, they know, but they are afraid to go after him. They will never arrest him. Manuel the tailor says he is going to report it to the governor. Who knows what will happen then!" [2]

Parsons listed a number of psychological attitudes "which . . . appeared . . . to partake of Indian rather than of European character," and among these were "fear of making enemies," and "unwillingness to give offense or make an enemy, which includes reticence about other people's affairs and unwillingness to take responsibility for anything which is not personally pressing." [3] In elaboration she wrote, ". . . In the affairs of your neighbor you do not interfere, you mind your own business, taking no initiative or responsibility that is not prescribed. Nor do you gossip lest what you say of anybody get reported to him and you make an enemy." She referred collectively to these feelings as an "Indian attitude of circumspection or prudence." [4]

But, like people the world over, Mitleños did not give equal weight to all of the rules they recognized. Any townsperson would say that people should not gossip, and would criticize other townspeople for being gossips. This was what Jerome Frank called a pretend rule: "All groups have their pseudo-standards, their 'pretend rules'; it is part of the rules of any group to break some of its own rules." [5] Our experience in Mitla proved beyond doubt that the injunction against gossip was a pseudo-standard, as indeed does Parsons' work, one of whose chapters is entitled "Town Gossip." But where the rule against interfering in other people's affairs was concerned, the correspondence between avowed ideal and actual practice was close.

Parsons interpreted the unwillingness of Mitleños to intervene in the disputes of others as an ancient Indian inheritance, "probably based on fear of the injury your enemy can work supernaturally." [6] The view

31

townspeople took of witchcraft is the subject of our next chapter. There we will show that witchcraft was commonly practiced in Mitla and that many townspeople feared its being used against them. But compared to other reasons for their insistence upon regarding acts of violence as private matters, fear of supernatural injury was a secondary concern of townspeople. These reasons were exceedingly practical, as a further discussion of the troublesome events related above will reveal.

The information that Pedro Santiago's son-in-law had been killed arrived while we were entertaining a number of neighbors at our house. They were amazed at the news, but they all knew immediately what would happen to the boys responsible for Margarito's death: they would run away to another town, and in a few weeks they would visit their homes secretly; then, in six months or a year, they would openly return to the community. They would not be arrested during their visits or later when they returned permanently. We were in Mitla when these events unfolded as predicted.

Similarly, on All Souls' when L. A. told us about the man R. J. stabbed, neither he nor his family expected R. J. to be arrested. They said that he would leave town for a few days, and when he returned he might have to pay the doctor's bill for his victim. And that was what happened.

The same pattern prevailed when Manuel Quero attempted to murder the tailor. But Manuel, not having killed or even wounded the tailor, "hid" in Mitla. This was an acknowledgment of his culpability but spared the authorities the task of arresting him. Even if he had exposed himself to arrest by remaining at home, he could only have been made to pay the damages for the tailor's horse, and possibly a small fine. He might also have been sentenced to one or two days in the town jail. But when he got out of jail he might have been more angry —now at the town officials as well as at the tailor!

Such are the considerations of townspeople, unwilling, as Parsons says, to "make an enemy, which includes . . . unwillingness to take responsibility for anything which is not personally pressing." With a wave of the hand our friends dismissed the competence of town officials to deal with really serious disputes. They made fun of the *topiles,* the young men whose office included police duty, by depicting them as incapable of arresting troublemakers because they were either paralyzed by fear or reeling drunk. These reputedly clumsy *topiles* were, in fact, very minor public officials. Townspeople considered the more responsible town officials to be capable of acting as arbitrators, but only in disputes where a few well-chosen words, a small fine, or a few days in jail will be efficacious. If a dispute was too serious to be handled in this way, they did not expect even these officials to attempt a local settlement or to resort to outside authorities.

When we encouraged friends to criticize the inaction of town officials when violence occurred, they said that the officials were prejudiced since some of their kinsmen were involved. The charge of prejudice, however, was made without bitterness or outrage, for no one expected office holders to be impartial in matters that touched their self-interest. It was, moreover, a conventionally simplified explanation that glossed over a difficult situation. Everyone recognized a whole complex of reasons why town officials did not appeal to outside authorities. Such action, first of all, would create one or more deadly enemies who might later seek revenge. Secondly, the officials would be humiliated by the outside authorities, who usually treated townspeople, including town officials, in a gruff and condescending manner. Thirdly, even if they risked humiliation by outside authorities and retaliation by local partisans, the outsiders would have so little knowledge of the community that they would be unable to appraise the situation—particularly when they were confronted with the lies and counter-lies that townspeople would tell them. Finally, townspeople were convinced that the outside authorities had little concern for their welfare and used their offices primarily to collect bribes.

What if Manuel the tailor, going over the heads of the town officials, took his case to the state authorities? As Parsons' friends observed, "Who knows what will happen then!" All our acquaintances in Mitla agreed that only one thing happened for certain in such cases. He would pay a bribe. And the more serious the affair and the more officials in-

33

volved, the more money it would cost him, and there would be no guarantee that these officials would not also accept bribes from his enemy.

A townsperson had to feel sure of himself and extremely spiteful to take his fight with another townsperson to state authorities. He would then be willing to pay the bribes and to suffer the humiliation of playing the role of a humble, ignorant villager to a powerful city person. Several times we heard stories about people who had done just this. They were funny stories in which the teller mimicked the exaggerated humility with which the agitated townsperson courted the official and paid a bribe, all to no purpose because the official never intended to take the action he promised or because he was also bribed by the person's antagonist. The moral of these anecdotes was that spiteful scheming led to ridiculous and self-defeating behavior. In the next chapter we will see how the same moral pervaded gossip about the attempts of townspeople to harm each other with witchcraft.

Townspeople were careful to avoid involvement in violent disputes because they recognized that there were no effective ways for controlling violence in their community. Individuals were not protected by the institutional machinery of criminal law. They believed that what little criminal law there was in the region was capriciously enforced by city people who possessed almost no understanding of or sympathy for their way of life. Secure only within his circle of kinsmen and friends, a townsperson looked out upon a dangerous world. It was most dangerous of all when he intruded into other communities, where he was not known and where neither family nor friends could help him if he got into trouble. Two Spanish words which townspeople often used, which are used all over Mexico, for that matter, were *conocido* (well-known) and *confianza* (confidence). A townsperson who made regular trading trips to other communities would say that he was *conocido* in such and such towns and that he had a relationship of *confianza* with individuals there. But for the most part a townsperson was only *conocido* in his home town, and it was within this community

34

that he was supported and protected by his relationship of *confianza* with kinsmen and friends.

It would not be correct to say that Mitleños *pretended* that violent outbreaks in their community were just private affairs between individuals, for in the absence of effective instruments of public law such outbreaks were in fact *particular*. But in their desire to feel civilized, they did pretend that violence was uncommon. They supported this pretense by comparing their community to what they believed were the practices of neighboring communities. In making such comparisons they clung to the persuasion that other towns were much rougher than their own, elaborating on evidence to this effect and discounting events which indicated otherwise.

Public Affairs and Political Unity

In a community where there are many conflicts between people and no efficient social machinery for settling these conflicts, the maintenance of a modicum of security by stalling the development of organized conflict becomes very important. Mitleños reminded themselves of the importance of maintaining a dispersion of conflicts within their town by their own vivid accounts of how political factions smouldered in neighboring towns, erupting occasionally in wholesale fighting, and afflicting people with chronic fear and suspicion. The length to which Mitleños went in order to avoid large-scale, organized civic strife can be illustrated by two episodes, one related by Parsons, the other observed by us.

While Parsons was in Mitla the state governor issued an order that the *presidente* was to be elected in a town meeting instead of appointed by the town council. A group of young men called a meeting and elected Don Rafael Toro *presidente*. The town council held another meeting at which one of their members, Carlos Sosa, was appointed to the same office. The governor sent a delegation headed by a deputy to investigate, and a meeting of townsmen was arranged in the plaza. But only one Mitleño spoke. "We are not divided," he announced; "there are no

35

parties in Mitla. We all want Carlos Sosa as president." The result, as reported by Parsons: "Within five minutes the assemblage began to disperse, and as the band played, the Deputy said to me with a smile, . . . 'If people always agreed together like these Mitleyenos we would have no trouble.' This was not the first or the last time I heard expressed by townspeople their standard of political unanimity. They know about political parties at Tlacolula and elsewhere . . . but they will have none of them." [7]

During our stay in Mitla, the *síndico,* an official second in authority to the *presidente,* was for months in bitter conflict over various matters with the *presidente* and other members of the town council. According to gossip, the *síndico* secretly sold title to a portion of land which had always been considered community property to a man from another town who had settled in Mitla. Other town officials maintained that the title was fraudulent, and that the *síndico* bribed the state official who came to Mitla to arbitrate the matter. The point for us is that throughout the controversies which swirled around the *síndico* and culminated in his loss of the office, townspeople of many different opinions about the case insisted that Mitla was politically unified, and that the *síndico*'s affairs were *particular.*

By denying the existence of any civic conflicts within their community, townspeople were not cynically saying one thing and believing something else. In the absence of effective institutional means for controlling social conflicts, they protected the community from large-scale violence, even to the point of classifying divisions among town officials and assaults on public property as private matters. Thus, the Mitleño refrain, "Now we are civilized," was something more than an incantation, although it was certainly that. Distance yawned between the ideal and the practice, but we have only to think of totalitarian societies, where disputes are only too liable to be classified as public, to realize that the Mitleño way of minimizing violence has its points.

IV. Witchcraft and Laughter

> The sense of the comic, the ability to laugh, is in him who laughs, and not at all in the object which excites his laughter . . . unless, that is, he . . . has acquired the power rapidly to become two persons at one and the same time, and can bring to bear on what happens to *himself* the disinterested curiosity of a spectator.
>
> —Charles Baudelaire [1]

Parsons referred to Mitla as a "witch-ridden community." [2] But strictly speaking this description was not accurate, at least not for Mitla in our time, for townspeople thought of witches as individuals who transformed themselves into animals. So far as we could determine, no townsperson had the reputation of being a witch in this, the Mitleño, sense. Those who professed a belief in witches asserted that Mitla used to produce such creatures but that they had entirely died out. One evening after we had discussed these matters at length with an elderly couple they observed that there had been much talk of witches in Mitla when they were children. "Now the style has changed," they said. Although they were expressing a popular opinion of townspeople, the opinion was also commonly expressed that other towns spawned witches, and these occasionally appeared in Mitla at night. Few townspeople seemed to fear these magical beasts, however.

And yet Mitla was indeed a town where witchcraft was practiced extensively. But it was practiced by ordinary people, not by supernaturals. Many townspeople employed curses (*maldades*) and other magical devices against their enemies, feared that these tactics would be used against them, and protected themselves with precautionary magic. They performed black magic by appealing to saints or to *ánimas solas,* the souls of people whose names had been forgotten. A saint's image, for instance, could be bound with cord and locked in a box with the admonition that it would not be freed until it had afflicted one's enemy, usually in a precisely specified way. Numerous charms were helpful in protecting the Mitleño from such vengeance, and if these failed he had recourse to professional curers, to herbs, and to the saints whom *he* petitioned. Parsons' book describes many of the items in the Mitleño repertoire of witchcraft. They are widespread in Mesoamerica and have been frequently reported. But what we are interested in is the place of witchcraft in the Mitleño world view, i.e., the kind of reality they attributed to it and the place it occupied in their mélange of beliefs and half-beliefs. In this respect what we immediately notice is that all their enterprise was riddled by doubts that witchcraft beliefs were true, and uncertainty whether black magic was involved in any particular incident of illness or misfortune.

There were townspeople who asserted that witchcraft was completely ineffective. Embarrassed by local beliefs and practices which they knew city people scorned, they were anxious not to appear credulous and simple-minded. Given the opportunity, they expressed their disdain of the curers who specialized in treating illnesses caused by magic, and ridiculed the popularity of protective charms.

But most townspeople were far more circumspect. They too wanted to avoid credulity and were quick to deride the gullibility of souls simpler than themselves. They laughed, for instance, at the malice of an individual who used black magic against an adversary. They referred to the body of beliefs concerning witchcraft as *creencias* (superstitions). They even occasionally imitated the assertive disbelievers and denounced witchcraft as absurdly futile. But privately they took precautions and in anger were sorely tempted to lay a curse upon the person who provoked them.

When we discussed witchcraft with townspeople they frequently stipulated that its magical formulas would not work unless one believed in them. Parsons recorded a similar proviso when her companion, Eligio Santiago, told her how a curer had once attributed an illness of his to witchcraft but had been unsuccessful in curing him. Eligio then went to another specialist: " 'Do you believe it is witchcraft?' she asked. 'No,' said Eligio. 'Believe, my son, and you can be cured, but only if you believe.' " [3]

Besides being uncertain about the reality of witchcraft, townspeople were frequently unsure whether or not it was relevant to a particular difficulty. Just as Eligio consulted several curers about his illness, other individuals with prolonged illnesses went from one specialist to another for different treatments, and not uncommonly for different diagnoses. An illness might be caused by witchcraft, or by a number of other things, and so long as a person continued to suffer he was receptive to a variety of interpretations of its cause.[4]

While townspeople of all shades of opinion about the reality of witchcraft acknowledged the popularity of its practice in their community, they did not think that Mitla was harassed by witchcraft in the manner suggested by Parsons' phrase, "witch-ridden community." They discounted witchcraft with laughter, by laughter exposing the freakishness of its formulas and the ridiculous distortion of character that accompanied an individual's surrender to spitefulness.

Witchcraft and Laughter

The humor of townspeople about witchcraft was not evoked by George Meredith's "comic spirit," with its refined and charitable insight into human foibles.[5] The comic view of witchcraft in Mitla had its characteristic expression in the unsympathetic laughter that Henri Bergson described when he wrote, "By laughter, society avenges itself for the liberties taken with it." [6] These liberties are nothing more or less than violations of common sense, which Bergson defines as "the endeavours of a mind continually adapting itself anew and changing ideas when it changes objects. It is the mobility of the intelligence conforming exactly to the mobility of things." Rather than behaving with common sense, a person may display "a certain rigidity of body, mind and character that society would like to get rid of in order to obtain from its members the greatest possible degree of elasticity and sociability. This rigidity is the comic, and laughter is its corrective." [7]

Whether or not Bergson's study of comedy is universally valid, he provides us with ideas which aid our understanding of the world view of Mitleños, for it is just the mental rigidity that characterized the vengeful anger of the person who practiced witchcraft, or the *idée fixe* of the individual who feared such magic, which provoked townspeople to laughter.

There were rich mimetic elements in the informal conversational style of townspeople, so that telling caricatures were achieved with gesture, and the Mitleño mime was abetted by the fact that almost everyone in town was known by a nickname which he was not himself supposed to know.[8] The satirist had subjects who were widely known by such names as *Crab Foot* (a townswoman with the habit of stretching and curling her toes), *Turtle* (a slow-moving townswoman with a short neck), *City Woman* (a townswoman whose vanity was revealed by her affectation of items of city clothing), *Marimba Teeth, Little Pig, Big Testicles.*

The imbroglios of people in a community in which nearly everyone was tagged by a nickname provided fellow townsmen with hilariously scandalous subjects of gossip, particularly when they engaged in unholy rituals of supernatural violence after having been duped in affairs of money and sex.

Before examining cases of this sort let us follow Bergson in describing "the kind of observation from which comedy springs." First, there is a suspension of those tender sentiments which flow from personal identification with another human being. Next, the comic view is "directed outwards" toward other people and away from the self. Finally, in its detached view of others, "comic observation instinctively proceeds to what is general. It chooses such peculiarities as admit of being reproduced and consequently are not indissolubly bound up with the individuality of a single person—a possibly common sort of un-commonness, so to say, peculiarities that are held in common." [9]

Bergson's description fits the manner in which our neighbors dis-cussed the predicament of La Tehuana. La Tehuana was a saucy, middle-aged woman who wore the long skirt and embroidered blouse of the Isthmus of Tehuantepec, which also furnished her nickname. She earned a living by selling gold jewelry made in the Isthmus and supported a lazy husband to whom she was devoted. Her husband fell ill and remained incapacitated for almost a year. He was even taken to the capital city for an operation. The burden of paying for the medi-cal expenses devolved on La Tehuana, who doubled her efforts as a merchant. Besides making frequent journeys to the Isthmus to buy jewelry, she travelled to markets and fairs all over the state. To take care of her house and husband while she was away she hired a young maid. One day La Tehuana returned and caught her husband making love to the maid. Her screams of rage resounded throughout the neigh-borhood. She fired the girl and browbeat her husband, but he soon left her to live with his new, younger, prettier and far more docile sweet-heart.

Furious with jealousy and desire for revenge, La Tehuana went into a frenzy of *maldades*. Every morning she feverishly lit evil-smelling candles of mutton grease before her household image of Jesús Nazareno and begged that her husband and the girl be struck with disease and misfortune. At noon she put the image in the blazing sun to burn as she would have her betrayers burn. Using thorns and wax images, dirt from the cemetery, playing cards and old photographs, La Tehuana practiced every device of black magic she knew. But all that happened was that once her former husband got drunk and fell on a rock which gashed his forehead.

La Tehuana's neighbors listened solemnly to her denunciations of her betrayers, but among themselves they laughed. They threw them-selves into rowdy imitations of her, and even ridiculed their own solemn demeanor when they listened to her imprecations. And yet on these same occasions they speculated seriously about the possibility that

La Tehuana's witchcraft had caused her husband to gash his head. In the peculiarities of La Tehuana's behavior there was "a possibly common sort of uncommonness."

Our neighbors took a similarly comic view of a controversy that developed between the wife of our next-door neighbor, Juan, and a widow across the street.[10] Teresa, Juan's wife, was convinced that he had been sleeping with the widow and told other neighbors that she had gone to Calvario to petition for revenge by burning candles behind the crosses.

In Mitla, widows were reputed to be particularly promiscuous, and, according to town lore, men lost their youth by having intercourse with older women. The widow in this affair was a lively, snaggle-toothed old woman nearly twice Juan's age, and Teresa was said to have caught them together in an uproarious scene in which Juan tried to hide under a blanket.

Having heard that Juan's wife was performing magic against her, the widow stood in the street one day and yelled insults at Teresa, who remained silently in her kitchen. The neighbors laughingly interpreted her refusal to answer insult for insult, as women sometimes did, as resulting from a caution not to weaken the curse she had laid on her rival.

The laughter of townspeople at such antics as those of La Tehuana, her husband and the maid, or of Juan, his wife and the widow, belonged to a public sphere of life. It was laughter in response to a view of social situations in which witchcraft had the appearance of a superstitious, uncertain and farcical complication. It was laughter at behavior that flaunted its moral and intellectual defects with ingenuous abandon. Using a phrase popular throughout the Spanish-speaking world, townspeople said that such behavior was "without shame."

Nevertheless, when the townsperson looked inward to his personal affairs the laughter dropped away, and witchcraft was seen as a possible means to revenge oneself on an enemy or as a threat to one's own welfare. Juan and his wife and the widow all laughed at La Tehuana, but they took their own affair seriously. Our landlady and her husband laughed at both of these affairs, but were angered and frightened when they discovered that someone was performing witchcraft against them. Our neighbors in turn laughed at our landlady's frantic efforts to counteract magic which she believed was being directed against her.

There was a great deal of small-town gossip in Mitla, and townspeople, who expected to spend their whole lives in the same small community, were quite concerned with the way their behavior would be reported and interpreted "in the street." The accusation that a person was "without shame" was a serious criticism. Though frequently made, it was perhaps most effective when it was accompanied by laughter.

Caught up in the fear and rage of witchcraft the townsperson acted "without shame." He did not see and he did not care that he was foolish—"The comic person is unconscious" [11]—but at other times when he looked out on *other* townspeople and saw them embroiled in bitter squabbles to the point of shameful practices, and when for a moment he grasped the absurdity of *their* loss of common sense, he laughed.

Not only was the reality of witchcraft challenged in Mitla, and not only was it conceived to be a vice, it was capable of appearing ridiculous. Since townspeople recognized it to be a source of comedy, and since they were sensitive to their appearance in the eyes of other townspeople and to the appearance of their community as a civilized town, there were in Mitla all of the ingredients for the educational process Bergson described in these words:

> . . . A defect that is ridiculous, as soon as it feels itself to be so, endeavours to modify itself or at least to appear as though it did. . . . Indeed, it is in this sense only that laughter "corrects men's manners." It makes us at once endeavour to appear what we ought to be, what some day we shall perhaps end in being.[12]

It is unlikely that the townsperson completely forgot or ignored or rationalized his own lapses into error when he laughed.

43

V. Conceptions of the Souls of Living People and of Sin

There was a popular belief in Mitla that an infant's soul had an exceedingly tenuous connection with its body. Sometime soon after a baby was born the mother tied an amulet to its wrist or ankle for the purpose of binding the soul to the body. Few children who were old enough to shift for themselves wore these amulets but small babies were rarely without them. Judging from this fact and from the testimony of townspeople with whom we discussed this custom, the common belief was that as the child grew in its ability to participate independently in social life, its soul became more securely ensconced. Still, the souls of young children were not as stable as those of adults, and mothers frequently put a few leaves of the pepper tree under their clothing when they were sent on errands or taken from the familiar surroundings of the household. The pungent odor of the leaves was said to serve the dual purpose of repelling witchcraft substances and of holding the soul close to the body.

The amulets were tied on children without formalities, and there was no particular time or ritual for later removing them or for replacing them if they were lost. Nor were pepper tree leaves secreted in the clothing with any ceremony. These practices, to use a phrase of Redfield's, were "without the benefit of the illuminating and explanatory formalisms which relate them to the moral life of the individual." [1]

45

The relatively deteriorated or superficial character of these practices was revealed by the fact that neither the amulet which bound the infant soul nor the aroma of the pepper tree leaves in the blouse of an older child was considered a powerful preventive of *mal ojo*, evil eye, the illness which resulted when a child's soul was dislodged from its body by the stare of strange people or animals.

Townspeople generally agreed that *mal ojo* was the most common malady of children, and parents usually attributed the deaths of their offspring to this cause. Yet there was general knowledge in the community that from the point of view of modern urban medicine this disease did not exist. The resident doctor in Mitla, who in accordance with state law filled out a certificate for every death in town, never missed an opportunity to make this known. Along with many other folk beliefs and practices in Mitla, the conception of *mal ojo* had gained the reputation among numerous townspeople of being a *creencia,* a rustic and even superstitious belief.

Yet infant mortality was high in Mitla so that there was good reason to fear for a child's life. And if one commonly heard that the souls of children were easily detached from the body, if the deaths of children were frequently laid to this cause, and if it was also said that the soul would be held by the odor of pepper tree leaves and by charms tied to the infant's wrists, then to observe such precautions was surely the prudent course of action. Founded on partial belief, motivated by fear, and lacking any profound meaning in the culture, it was a debased course of action. Perhaps a few individuals saw this with clarity, but for most townspeople it was an obscure perception that appeared and slipped from consciousness when they emulated the sophistication of city people and referred to these soul-securing practices patronizingly as *costumbres,* quaint ways of the local community. At the funeral of a neighboring child, for instance, everyone seemed to agree that the death was caused by *mal ojo.* But later one of our neighbors told us that it was a *costumbre* of ignorant people to say that their children died of *mal ojo.* In this case, confided our friend, the baby had sickened and died because the mother's anger, when she discovered that her

46

husband had been having an affair with another woman, had passed into her milk! [2]

A common illness of adults which resulted from loss of soul was called *espanto,* or *susto,* fright. Just as children might lose their souls when they ventured into strange surroundings or when strangers intruded upon their familiar world, adults also incurred this risk when the ordinary routine of their lives was suddenly interrupted. For example, if a person came upon a snake unexpectedly or was startled by a vicious dog, the sudden fright might jar the soul from the body. If this happened the symptoms of *espanto* would eventually appear. These symptoms were commonly loss of appetite, nausea, lassitude, and fever. When a specialist diagnosed an illness as *espanto,* the patient underwent private rituals for calling the soul back to the body. The curer called upon several saints for help, but no one believed that the afflicted person was morally responsible for his sickness, and, just as his symptoms did not include any moral alteration of his behavior, so the treatment did not require him to make any moral commitments. *Espanto,* in short, was a magical affliction and it was cured by magical incantations which lured the soul back to the body. In it and in the concern townspeople showed for the souls of children, the soul appeared thinglike: it was devoid of moral qualities, the subject simply of mechanical dislocations.

Sin and the Soul

In the following chapter we will see that the souls of dead people who had made their transition to the afterlife were sacred to their kinsmen. On certain occasions this transition was not immediately accomplished, however, and these occasions reveal the way that townspeople modified Catholic notions of purgatory and of sin to fit their conception of the souls of living people and their mildly hedonistic view of the good life. The manner in which they modified these Catholic notions can be illustrated most concretely by recounting an episode which occurred during our residence in Mitla.

47

In early January of 1954 a young man named Severiano was killed in the Mixe-speaking town of Zacatepec. He had lived on different occasions with a widow and with the family of a male friend. The sister of his friend was said to be his sweetheart, and the widow was supposed to be his mistress. Severiano had gone to Zacatepec with some Mitleño friends who had been hired to play the marimba at a wedding. While his companions were playing at the wedding he joined an acquaintance who invited him to have a drink at a local store. They were drinking when another man entered the store with the intention of killing Severiano's acquaintance, but in the melee he also shot Severiano.[3]

Severiano's mistress and his sweetheart asserted that they had known that he was dead even before the marimba players returned with the news. The widow had seen the ghostly image of Severiano standing in the doorway of her house, and the sister of Severiano's friend had heard his invisible spirit rattle a wooden chest. These were signs that Severiano was suffering from a *mala muerte*, bad death. When we asked a friend what exactly was meant by *mala muerte*, he imitated Severiano's dying moments, explaining that in the shock, the physical jerk and gasp of sudden death, the soul was torn from the body. We had seen and heard similar descriptions earlier when another townsman was accidentally killed.

When death came slowly enough for the dying person and his family to expect that it was coming, there was grief but not the terror of *mala muerte*. Under these circumstances the soul left the body in a normal manner, aided by the incense that filled the room in which death occurred. The proper attitude toward such a death was one of resigned acceptance, often expressed in the observation that, just as candles of different sizes burned for longer or shorter periods, so the lives of individuals had various determined lengths. But the soul of a person who died abruptly became an *alma en pena*, an afflicted soul that could not complete its transition to the other world. This idea did not, however, conform to the Catholic conception of purgatory. The soul experiencing the *pena*, pain, consequent to sudden death was not

A funeral procession for an angelito.

A religious procession, part of a mayordomía, *or saint's celebration.*

A family from a mountain town near Mitla.

Decorating the graves for All Souls'.

Guelagueza, *the ritual exchange of food and other goods at saints celebrations.*

A prayer image made at the cross on a hill near Mitla on New Year's Eve.

atoning for sin; it was simply harassed by the compulsion to complete the expectations and obligations that death had interrupted. Townspeople said of such a person, "His time had not yet arrived." Severiano's spirit returned, as he had expected to do, to his sweetheart and mistress in Mitla.

The *pena* of a soul could result from events other than murders and fatal accidents. A family we knew rushed to have a sick baby baptized when they thought that it would die. If they had allowed it to die "like an animal," unbaptized, it would suffer *pena* which it would try to relieve by causing the death of one of the responsible people. Any person whose death could have been prevented might suffer *pena* for which he would seek revenge and relief among those who were responsible. Also, if the family did not properly conduct a funeral the soul of the dead person would experience *pena* and seek revenge.

In her analysis of acculturation, Parsons emphasized the absence of the Christian doctrine of sin in Mitla. At the same time she observed that townspeople did not think of heaven and hell as places where they would be rewarded or punished for their terrestrial conduct.[4] Our next chapter will discuss the way in which townspeople conceived of the existence of souls that had completed their transition to the other world. All we need to say at this point is that in Catholic prayers the Spanish terms for sin, purgatory, heaven and hell were constantly mentioned, but that townspeople attached their own meanings to these words. The Spanish term for hell, for instance, was usually rendered into Zapotec as *gabihl,* which designated a realm of the dead coexistent with this world in which the souls lived much as they lived during their lifetimes. According to townspeople, any person who *really* died, and whose soul made its transition to the afterlife, lived in this "hell." They did describe the domain of the devil-who-gave-wealth as a hellish *hacienda* where his victims worked constantly, were beaten, and had only wheat bread to eat. But, according to this lore, the captives of the devil only appeared to die, and many of them were innocent servants of wealthy people. As we have seen in an earlier chapter, gossip about the devil-who-gave-wealth was a way of criticizing the conduct of rich people. It was not a way townspeople imagined their own destiny after death. Similarly, townspeople did not conceive of heaven as a dwelling place of the souls. It was for them a vague, far-away place in the sky where God and some saints lived.

Of course townspeople had heard explanations of the Christian meaning of these terms, but few of them were impressed with the explanations. Perhaps at funerals more than at any other time they were reminded of the doctrine that immorality resulted in a soul heavy with sin. And funeral ceremonies include lengthy rituals to relieve the soul of its burden of sin. But the notion of sin possessed little or no moral resonance, for townspeople interpreted literally such terms as "heavy" and "burden." Thus, the custom was to bury people without metal on their clothing or bodies. And during the wake the corpse was laid on the floor on a cross of quicklime which was said to lighten the body by reducing the weight of sin. If a corpse was heavy when it was carried to the cemetery, then the dead person was supposed to have the weight of his sins still upon him. But this misfortune might be due to the negligence of those who conducted the funeral, or to a *mala muerte* for which the dead person was scarcely responsible.

In the light of the foregoing, it is hardly surprising that townspeople conducted themselves in everyday affairs with little if any attention to the possibility that illicit behavior would provoke supernatural punishment. In Parsons' judgment, ". . . There is much less feeling about automatic sanctions at Mitla than in many Indian communities." [5] Our observations confirmed those of Parsons that Mitleños prayed "for material benefits, for health, long life, crops . . . wealth, [and] for revenge," and that "ideas of moral or spiritual welfare are negligible" in their prayers. [6] As far as we could determine, townspeople did not pray for supernatural help to achieve a more virtuous life.

During saints' celebrations, weddings and funerals—all occasions for heavy drinking and hours of friendly conversation—townspeople expounded to us at length their opinion that in this world of pain and error we should forgive ourselves and others for seeking pleasure however we can. An elderly friend of ours once explained that he was old and close to death but that it would not be difficult for him to die because he had had his share of alcohol, women and festivals. But the man who denied himself these delights, he continued, would want liquor and music when he was dying, and his feet would twitch with the desire to dance. Townspeople used the word "sinner" as an epithet for the person with minor vices and the great virtue of being a lively companion.[7] In Mitla, as in many other parts of the world, the statement, "We are all sinners," was a favorite expression of camaraderie.

VI. The Souls of the Dead and the Saints

. . . Living faith . . . is in need of miracles.
　　　　　—Bronislaw Malinowski [1]

After death and transition to the realm of the afterlife the soul assumed divine qualities in the eyes of townspeople. Throughout the year individuals prayed to their dead kinsmen for supernatural aid. Believing that dead children had not lived long enough to learn the customs of the community, they addressed their prayers to the souls of adults.

From the moment of death the soul was supposed to watch its kinsmen to see that they were genuinely grieved and that they performed their obligations to it correctly. We have already reported lore which is widely quoted among townspeople that a dead person revenged himself upon his family if they had neglected him while he was dying, or grudged the expense of the funeral, or quarreled over the inheritance. This lore included various omens of the dead person's anger: the church bells which announced the death might toll with ominous emphasis; the eyes of the corpse might not close; the corpse might be extraordinarily heavy when it was carried to the cemetery; finally, there might not be enough dirt to fill the grave when it was packed with a pounding stone.

After death, the soul was said to remain for a time in the house of death. Candles and flowers, together with water with which the soul might refresh itself, were kept near a lime cross on the floor in front of the house altar where the corpse was laid out for the wake. While the soul was immediately present, it was also said to be engaged in a journey to the realm of the other world. A small cloth bag containing food and water for this journey was fastened to the shroud, and after the burial, which followed a twenty-four-hour wake, the family and close friends began a novena. On the ninth night they prayed until the early hours of the morning and then took the lime that formed the cross, the flowers and the candles to the cemetery. This ceremony, which townspeople called "the raising of the cross," was supposed to complete the soul's transition to the world of the dead.

As one would expect in a heterogeneous community, there were variations among the funerals we attended—sometimes the corpse was taken to the church for a mass, or the lime cross was elaborated into a sand painting for the novena, or "the raising of the cross" was performed twenty days after the burial—but these variations did not lessen the always impressive simplicity and vividness with which townspeople imagined the presence of the soul and its transition to the nether world. During funerals there was heavy drinking, and many people lurched through the ceremonies in an alcoholic stupor. This drunkenness mixed with the funeral odor of incense and flowers to create an atmosphere of oppressive tension, and the world of appearances pulsed with the terrible mystery of death. During the novena for her husband a widow reported that she felt the dead man lying beside her at night, and other townspeople who were present commented that this was not unusual. Similarly, members of bereaved families frequently reported that they saw objects move and that they heard noises as the soul gathered the essences of its belongings to take to the other world.

Although funeral ceremonies were weighty with supernatural portents, the streets and the market hummed with gossip: Was the family quarreling about the inheritance? Was the widow already thinking of sleeping with another man? Was the corpse heavy? How much food was bought to serve the mourners? There was piety throughout the community at only one time during the year, and that was during All Souls'. On All Souls' the dead formally visited with their living relatives and received offerings that would sustain them during the coming year. Everywhere in the town families engaged in a prayerful relationship with their dead kinsmen.

The tempo of life came to a great climax in preparation for the return of the dead on All Souls'. The variety and quality of goods in the daily market increased, and people swarmed to buy and sell. On weekends townspeople crowded into the buses to Tlacolula and Oaxaca, where they bought new clothes to wear to welcome the souls, and new pottery and baskets to contain their offerings of food. When All Souls' arrived, the streets emptied, the town seemed deserted, and the endlessly tolling church bells echoed from yard to yard. In their homes families quietly, respectfully communed with their dead.

Townspeople recounted numerous miracles performed by the souls during their annual visitations. They reported these miracles with intimate details, and characteristically prefaced or concluded their accounts by saying, "This is the pure truth, it happened to a man who died several years ago"; "This is certain, it happened to my father"; "I saw this myself and know that it is true." Fausto Raimundo, for example, told us the story of Juana of Santa María, who had lived in our neighborhood in the autumn of 1952. Juana was poor and worked hard for townspeople who hired her to grind corn for their offerings on All Souls'. But she confided to her neighbor that she did not plan to prepare her own altar with offerings because none of her family had died in Mitla. Her neighbor worried about Juana's neglect of the souls, and on the morning of All Souls' took some ritual food to Juana for her altar. Exhausted from many days of toil, Juana laid the food to one side and sat down to rest, but in a moment she was paralyzed by a trance. The souls of her father and mother entered her hut, accompanied by one of Juana's dead Mitleña friends. When they saw that the altar was barren they were bitterly disappointed and said that they would have to go elsewhere. Emerging from her trance, Juana cried out, but the souls were already gone. A few months later Juana died.

Townspeople told numerous anecdotes similar to the one about Juana. Another story which circulated in many versions concerned

55

the soul of a man who had been a drunkard during his mundane career. Offended when he did not find liquor among his relatives' offerings on All Souls', he rattled their altar with such violence that he knocked over all of the offerings which were not to the point. A third kind of story enjoyed a similar popularity: A dying Mitleño, bent on testing the belief that the souls returned on All Souls', promised his family to move the bread set out for him if he visited them the following year. The experiment was a robust success, for the following year two loaves were mysteriously tossed from the altar.

Though a "living faith . . . is in need of miracles," accounts such as these tended to become formulas to sustain a belief in the souls that lacked the ultimate spontaneous leap of religious faith. The relationship of townspeople with the dead was characterized by a blend of religious awe and familiarity, of morality and self-seeking, of spiritual reverence and supernatural dread which was reminiscent of Huizinga's description of the religious life of the late Middle Ages. In such a religion, according to Huizinga, there is "a dangerous state of tension, for the presupposed transcendental feelings are sometimes dormant, and whenever this is the case, all that is meant to stimulate spiritual consciousness is reduced to appalling commonplace profanity, to a startling worldliness in other-worldly guise." [2]

The "worldliness in other-worldly guise," which occasionally appeared in the Mitleño conception of the souls, was not always as simple as in the miracles which testified to the actual return of the dead on All Souls'. For example, with the usual assurances that it was a true account of events well known to the speaker, we were told a tale quite similar to one recorded by Parsons in which a townsman cautioned his wife "to take good care of the money" while he was away on a trading trip. His wife dutifully hid the money, but died before her husband's return. When he learned what had happened he was disconsolate and began to drink heavily. He was drunk one night when an owl cast a spell over him and transported him to the nether world where he met his wife in the company of another man. Surprised, she asked him why he had come. "Wife, I have come to see you because

I love you very much and because I want you to tell me where you hid the money." She told him the hiding place and went on her way with the other man. Her husband watched jealously to see where they went, and then set fire to the house. Emerging from the spell he was under, he discovered that he had burned his own house.

In this tale, as it was told both to us and to Parsons, the avarice and drunken jealousy of the husband were thinly justified by his purported grief for his dead wife and by his avowal of love when he encountered her in the other world. Although the story as we heard it had the same quality as much comical gossip about living townspeople, the ostensible reason for telling it was to give evidence of the way of life of the souls.[3]

Nevertheless, the usual attitude of townspeople toward the souls was worshipful, and the rituals of All Souls' and of funerals provided occasions upon which they transcended the ordinary experiences of their lives. Moreover, the reverent manner in which individuals prayed to the souls ennobled their lives. For example, after preparing an offering of food, candles, and flowers, a man would address his dead parents with tender respect, "Father, Mother, I am going to Zacatepec to buy coffee. My *compadre* Lencho has given me 1,500 pesos of corn and other things to take with me to sell. Help me to make good sales and good purchases, and to return in twenty days with all my mules and burros well. I want to build another room on my house; if this trip goes well I will have the money. When I come back I will buy a candle for you and pay for a response." [4] The piety of such occasions counterbalanced the worldly dissonances that marked the confrontation of townspeople with the souls.

The Saints

Townspeople prayed to the saints and to the souls, and it was to them, not to God, that they attributed miraculous events. They characteristically thought of the saints as objects with supernatural powers. Literally, the saints were the carved, the painted and the printed images in churches and on the altars of their homes. Most saints, they pointed out, were bought in stores or at fairs, but the most powerful images made miraculous appearances in the communities where they were presently located. In the accounts townspeople gave of these miraculous appearances the image was sometimes said to have been appointed to a particular locality by God, but more often the teller implied that the image was self-created and that it arbitrarily chose the place where it wanted a shrine built in its honor. Mitla possessed such an image—San Pablo, the patron of the community. And yet when townspeople told the story of his appearance they abbreviated the details and spoke with less enthusiasm than when they recounted the miraculous appearance of the image of San Antonio in Santa Catarina Albarrados. And there were images in two other towns to which they attributed greater power than they did to their own patron. Besides the San Antonio in Santa Catarina Albarrados, there was the Virgen de los Remedios in nearby Matatlán, and in the distant town of Juquila, the Virgen de Juquila, to all of which a number of Mitleños made annual pilgrimages. In large part townspeople considered these pilgrimages as occasions for engaging in profitable trade, and for enjoying the bull riding, the displays of fireworks, the dances and other secular entertainments provided by the host communities. With the air of dilettantes they referred to the fact that in different towns different pilgrimages were stylish, and that among themselves the pilgrimage to Santa Catarina had recently acquired great popularity, while the pilgrimage to Juquila was becoming less fashionable. In 1954 the town officials advertised the celebration for the patron saint of Mitla by distributing circulars to neighboring communities. The circulars announced the amusements and commercial opportunities visitors would find at the fair, but did not mention San Pablo by name, nor the special masses that would be said in his honor.

Also, in the strictly local saints' festivals—the *mayordomías*—the veneration of the saints was subordinated to secular diversions. *Mayordomías* began with a novena at the *mayordomo*'s home that culminated on the saint's day when the *mayordomo* went to the church and paid for a mass. But few of the guests invited to participate in a *mayor-*

domía attended the novena or the special mass in honor of the saint. All, however, joined in the festival banquets and dances which followed. These gay affairs sometimes lasted a whole week—as long, in fact, as the liquor and food held out and there were funds to pay the musicians.

We frequently discussed with townspeople the way a man decided to sponsor a *mayordomía*. They always emphasized that in the past the town officials could require a man to become a *mayordomo*, so that many times there was no choice as to which saint an individual would pay homage to, or the year in which he would undertake this "burden." The newer, and by general agreement the better, arrangement was for the prospective *mayordomo* to choose voluntarily the *mayordomía* he would sponsor. Even so, every man was still expected to sponsor two *mayordomías* as a part of his town service, and individuals who postponed fulfilling this expensive obligation were bitterly criticized throughout the community. If no one volunteered to replace the *mayordomo* for a particular saint the town officials formally requested individuals to take the office. A man could refuse such requests only with excuses that became more and more embarrassing as time passed.

A few men openly depreciated the *mayordomías*, maintaining that these festivals were economically wasteful for the whole community, a burden that had financially ruined a number of families, and that they were not genuinely religious. Some of these men suggested that the saints' days be celebrated with no more than a mass. But even these critics went ahead and sponsored traditional *mayordomías* in order to avoid a reputation for shirking their responsibilities to the community.

Townspeople who looked upon the *mayordomías* as a good thing also emphasized their costs and the difficulty these costs imposed upon the *mayordomo* and his family. They described the way a man, aided by his wife and the other members of his family, worked hard and saved his earnings in order to finance his festival. Particularly, they described with warm approval the *guelagueza* system of exchange in accordance with which the future *mayordomo* and his wife attended as many festivals as they could in the period before their own festival.

On these occasions they brought gifts of money, food and liquor. These gifts were carefully recorded by their hosts, who were then obliged to return them in kind when they were later invited to the festivals of their guests. The prospective *mayordomo* accumulated these obligations among his friends until he had enough to undertake his own festival. But he also invited people to his celebration who did not owe him *guelagueza*, so that he finished his *mayordomía* in debt.

The decision to sponsor a saint's festival involved primarily economic rather than religious considerations. Nevertheless, these calculations were of a different order from those in ordinary economic exchanges, which were conducted for profit and were felt to be constantly threatened by every device of misrepresentation at the command of buyer and seller, lender and borrower. Most townspeople were deeply engaged in the two systems of economic exchange: confined to members of the community, the *guelagueza* system, from which the profit motive was excluded and the goal was to cooperate in financing festivals which honored the community-owned saints; and, linking Mitleños to the outside world as well as to each other, the market system, in which the profit motive combined with fluctuating prices to encourage an impersonal, bitterly competitive scramble for advantage. Bargaining and lying were the order of the day in the market, but *guelagueza* exchanges were perfectly reciprocal, and they were conducted with many graceful formalities. Understandably, townspeople saw superior moral qualities in the *guelagueza* system, but religious piety was not one of these virtues. The *guelagueza* system was extolled because it was a means by which townspeople trustfully aided their kinsmen and friends to perform a difficult part of their services to the community.

Economic motives also powerfully influenced a man's decision as to which saint's celebration he would undertake. The celebrations for some saints were traditionally larger and more expensive than others, and wealthier townsmen were expected to sponsor these *mayordomías,* while poorer townsmen usually selected one of the images with a reputation for smaller festivals. Other motives were also recognized—a

60

mayordomo's choice might be determined by the fact that other images had already been spoken for—but, significantly, in all of our discussions about the choice of saints by *mayordomos,* religious motives were not emphasized, and frequently they were ignored altogether.

According to town gossip even scandalous motives occasionally entered into the decision of a townsperson to sponsor a saint's celebration. This was the case when La Tehuana paid for a mass and held a small festival for Jesús Nazareno on the fifth Friday of Lent. From an earlier chapter we may recall La Tehuana's unsuccessful witchcraft against her former husband. She and her husband had once sponsored the *mayordomía* for Jesús Nazareno, but a political disturbance throughout the state forced them to curtail their festival. Soon afterwards La Tehuana's husband became severely ill. She used up all their savings on medical treatments, but when her husband recovered he left her for another woman. Her neighbors said that La Tehuana was convinced that her bad luck was caused by the vengefulness of the saint, and that she hoped her witchcraft would be more effective after she appeased the image with a mass and second festival.

Townspeople were convinced that individuals frequently treated the saints in a scandalous manner. They said that individuals compelled saints to lay curses on their enemies, a result which they achieved by putting images of the saints in the mid-day sun to burn, or binding them and imprisoning them in boxes, or suspending them in the darkness of water wells. And some Mitleños, it was asserted, were such habitual liars they even tried to mislead the saints with falsehoods similar to those they told in the market place. In addition, it was a scandalous commonplace in Mitla that individuals went to the church to petition the saints for aid in illicit sexual affairs, or for success in stealing.

The Souls and the Saints

Although there was some "worldliness in other-worldly guise" in the way townspeople viewed the souls, their view of the saints was by comparison far more worldly, and this worldliness was often concealed by

61

merely perfunctory religious gestures. Most townspeople recognized the irony of the critics of the *mayordomía* system who suggested that the saints' festivals should be reduced to their religious elements. These critics were not, and did not claim to be, more pious than other people —their suggestion was ironic because townspeople assumed but did not ordinarily like to admit that the worship of the saints was a relatively minor purpose of the *mayordomías*. As a part of the system of town service and as a way of demonstrating to the community one's wealth and generosity, the *mayordomías* were primarily a means of affirming the status of the *mayordomo* and his family, and of expressing the solidarity of the community. In addition, they were rowdy entertainments at which an abundance of food and liquor helped people to forget for awhile the pressing and difficult problems of earning a living.

Noting that "the whole domain of ghost-seeing, signs, spectres and apparitions, so crowded in the Middle Ages, lies mainly apart from the veneration of the saints," Huizinga suggested, "It may well be that this too corporeal and familiar aspect, this too clearly outlined shape, of the saints has been the very reason why they occupy so little space in the sphere of visions and supernatural experience." [5] The religious system Huizinga was describing was more complex, mystical and intense than that of Mitla, but in Mitla, too, the saints were less mysterious and awesome powers than other, less corporeal supernatural beings. Even skeptical townspeople occasionally succumbed to the eerie attraction of anecdotes about the encounters of individuals with diabolical spirits that were supposed to haunt the landscape in the forms of seductive women and frolicsome children, and many townspeople described with fascinated voices the fabulous devil-who-gave-wealth. Moreover, there were constant references in Mitla to such bits of lore as the sound of a phantom cart, the wailing of a feminine spectre, or the appearance of a supernatural owl as omens of death. It is difficult to say just how much belief this lore commanded. It evidently provided townspeople with a number of conventional and gratifyingly familiar landmarks in the uncertain realm of the supernatural. On the other hand, we occasionally encountered a suggestion of skepticism. One evening, for example, when a group of townspeople had swapped anecdotes of weird experiences for several hours, swearing each tale to be true, a sagacious old man began his account of an experience of his *compadre* by saying, "I know this is true because it happened in the day time and not at night!"

Shadowy and frequently threatening, the miraculous powers of the dead souls were fully accepted by townspeople. Fausto Raimundo concluded his account of how the death of Juana of Santa María had resulted from her neglect of the souls, by saying, "We are forced to adorn our altars; this is something everyone here believes." And this belief contributed to a larger attitude of religious awe which, on the whole, distinguished the confrontation of townspeople with the souls from their confrontation with other supernaturals.

Relative to the souls, the saints lacked supernatural mystery, and relative to the mysterious supernatural creatures that lurked in the vicinity of Mitla and neighboring towns, the souls were divine. This was so even though the legendary accounts of a period before the sun arose, in which Mitla became the center of the world of the dead, had lost much of their meaning for townspeople. The tradition of the town of the souls appeared anachronistic as well as fanciful to most townspeople. Members of a self-consciously changing community which was committed to an image of itself as a "civilized" town, they associated that tradition with their "Indian" past. Although the miraculous events of the legendary past had lost connection with present-day reality, the living faith of townspeople was still in need of miracles—miracles suited to a reality in which seeing was believing. Yet these miracles were rarely supposed to occur in the broad daylight or to people who were sober and in good health. Perhaps they too were nearing a threshold beyond which the laughter of the street would echo its ridicule —"Wife, I have come to see you because I love you very much and because I want you to tell me where you hid the money."

Our impression was that the souls were more sacred to townspeople than the saints because they were more intimately and permanently related to individuals than were the saints. It was not the souls in general that a townsperson worshipped, but the souls of his close kinsmen. So long as he performed his obligations to them they would not turn upon him, and, since they belonged to the miraculous realm of the dead, they could give him supernatural aid. Townspeople maintained that no one could for a moment succeed in lying to the souls, and, although the anonymous souls of people long dead and forgotten could be appealed to for revenge upon an enemy, if such a petition was not morally justified these spirits might very well scourge the petitioner. The saints, on the other hand, were impersonal powers, and susceptible to blasphemous treatment.

Thus, the souls belonged to the private sphere of an individual's personal relations. Within this sphere townspeople were firmly convinced that their ideals of honesty, generosity, respectfulness and responsibility were practical as well as intrinsically good. They realized these virtues to a significant degree in acts of piety toward the souls of their dead kinsmen. In contrast, the saints belonged primarily to the public sphere of community relations where ethical ideals were so frequently violated that piety not infrequently appeared to be a manifestation of naivete or of hypocrisy. We never heard anyone in Mitla speak disparagingly of another person's piety toward the souls, but occasionally a townsperson mocked somebody's display of devotion to the saints, or described with mixed condescension and sympathy what he considered to be an overly humble veneration of the saints on the part of naive individuals. Even women who visited the church unusually often were liable to figure in town gossip nicknamed as mistresses of the priest.

We have devoted this and the preceding chapter to those supernatural entities encompassed by the world view of most Mitleños— living souls, dead souls, saints, and that miscellany of supernatural manifestations which comprised the minor items of folklore. The veneration of the dead fused religion and morality to a greater extent than the other activities of townspeople. Worshipping a dead soul was one of those intimate, familial matters in respect to which morality made the most sense to a Mitleño. The veneration of saints, on the other hand, was colored by the overtly secular and ironic view townspeople adopted toward public issues and events. The *mayordomías,* around which much of the communal life in Mitla revolved, paid homage to the saints, and yet the saints were outside that circle of kinsmen and close friends within which moral obligation was rooted in the heart and conscience.

VII. The Acquisitive Society

Such societies may be called Acquisitive Societies, because their whole tendency and interest and preoccupation is to promote the acquisition of wealth.

—R. H. Tawney [1]

"Price, price, price!" exclaimed Elsie Clews Parsons. "Instead of a ritual, a price list! A ritual of price!" [2] Our observations of this aspect of life in Mitla confirm those of Parsons:

Mitla is a business town. Trade permeates its whole life; price is of supreme interest to young and old, women and men, the poor and the well-to-do. The expression of this interest is very direct, and from our point of view quite shameless. . . . At first I inferred that this incessant questioning about the price of things was due to the novelties a stranger presented. Questions about unfamiliar goods or experiences almost always began or ended with a money valuation; but then I noted that familiar experience was rated in the same way and that the price of familiar goods was inquired about with just the same kind of interest. . . . I noticed, too, that Mitleyenos would relate their own experience abroad in money terms. . . . Money cost enters into the evaluation of things and of experience to a degree I have never found equaled in any other society, including the most plutocratic circles. [3]

In Chapter I of the present work we compared Mitleños to villagers in Guatemala who were "perhaps above all else" entrepreneurs, and, noting their enthusiasm for the bustle of the market place, we observed that they found the most obvious confirmation of the notion that they were civilized in the lively commercial activity of their town. In subsequent chapters we examined other aspects of the meaning of civilization to townspeople, but we have yet to consider in some detail their preoccupation with pecuniary values.

The Reality of the Market Place

Nothing seemed to enter the minds of our friends more spontaneously and with a greater sense of reality or appropriateness than the thought of money. The language associated with money helped individuals express themselves under the most diverse circumstances. We may recall the devout prayer of a townsman to his dead parents, in which he told them of a 1,500-peso loan he would use to go on a trading journey, and in return for their aid promised to buy them a candle and to pay for a response. In an altogether different context, one of our neighbors resorted just as naturally and automatically to monetary considerations. Denounced as a whore by her sister-in-law, she answered by shouting that she had men for pleasure whereas her adversary was a whore for money.

Our friend Pedro Santiago drew our attention to the paved highway, which increased commerce in town, and recalled a prolonged drought during his youth when "hunger walked the streets and even city people ate maguey. Now, when there is a drought there is a road, and there are airplanes to bring food from far away. Only, how are we to get money to buy it?" His question was not really a question—from an image of planes bringing corn to the drought-stricken valley he immediately, and, for a townsperson, characteristically returned to the fact that the scarcity of pesos would still be a problem.

The possibility of hunger constituted the most obvious and compelling reason for the Mitleño's concern for money. Thus, Pancho Quero, a corn merchant, compared Mitla favorably with neighboring towns because its stores contained a wide choice of manufactured goods, because meat, bread and fresh vegetables could be bought in

68

the daily market, and because townspeople kept their clothing and houses in good repair. But at the same time he cautioned us to realize that many families in Mitla were frequently worried about how to get enough food to satisfy their hunger.

The possibility of hunger was deeply embedded in the imaginative life of the community. A youth described with great feeling a famine which was supposed to have occurred years before he was born. The fear of starvation had been fixed in his consciousness by the accounts of his elders. And current in the folk medicine of Mitla is an illness which results from the intense desire of a person to eat something he has seen but been unable to have. The symptoms of this malady are said to be peculiar stomach growls and pains. If an afflicted person has seen and wanted turkey, explained the brother of this same youth, "his stomach will make noises like the noise of a turkey when it wakes up at dawn and ruffles its wings." [4]

But, powerful in fact and imagination as was the threat of hunger, it provided only one of the motives which stimulated the obsessive concern of townspeople with money. We have already seen that each adult man was expected to serve in a number of town offices. During the periods in which a man was working for the community he was unable to occupy himself fully with making a living. Consequently, he had to accumulate the means to hold town offices. Since he was also expected to sponsor two saints' celebrations during his adult career, he was obliged to save considerable sums for these festivities. Added to this were the expenses of weddings and funerals, and the cost of meeting local standards of decently clean and presentable dress.

Such were the minimal expectations of the community. Then there was a multiplicity of private household expenses—purchases of cooking utensils, candles, baskets, sleeping mats. Households that managed somehow to meet all demands, public and private, were left with few reserves to overcome the financial losses caused by illnesses.

Finally, townspeople strove to acquire wealth simply because they enjoyed material well-being, and because prestige was gained by wearing clothing that was stylish as well as decent, by maintaining a household that was well-equipped, and by lavishing one's means on festivals.

Mitleños had to achieve their purposes in an economy where both the price and the quality of goods constantly fluctuated. From one transaction to another, from season to season and year to year, individuals experienced the uncertainty of market transactions. This uncertainty was primarily due to the shifts in supply and demand, but it was aggravated by the fact that the market place was a grand arena in which townspeople practiced the art of lying.

The rhetoric of the market place followed the rules for lying outlined in an earlier chapter. (See pages 26–27.) Buyer and seller matched wits in estimating the other's need and desire to complete an exchange. The poker face, the assumption of nonchalance, the strategy of the opening bid—these were the elementary gambits with which the game started. Sellers proclaimed the health and vigor of animals they believed to be sick, and, in general, the soundness and high quality of anything they knew to be defective. Buyers, on the other hand, discovered imaginary flaws in the products they wanted, and feigned amazement at reasonable prices. Such dissimulation combined every device of misrepresentation, flattery or insult which the ingenuity of the actors could turn to their advantage.

Our friends to a man condemned the roguery of the market place. They said that such behavior was "without shame," but they saw opportunities in it for financial gain, and, unless they were personally harmed or someone had scandalously violated a relationship of confidence, they were more amused than offended by incidents of it.

Although individuals told us how other townspeople had cheated them, we cannot recall anyone admitting to us that he had cheated another Mitleño. On the other hand, a popular kind of joke was one in which a townsperson recounted the way that he or a friend had fleeced an outsider, particularly a Mixe-speaking villager from the mountains. These anecdotes, along with tales which were considered fictional, made economic deception a game of epic dimensions. For example, the hero of one of the stories of a kind Mitleños told for amusement during festivals begins his career by taking the fine white horse a priest has recently purchased and, darkening its coat with mud, selling it to the cleric a second time. Then, in the subsequent episodes of a long journey, he sells another man's pigs to an unsuspecting merchant and substitutes gravel for corn in the bags of some muleteers.

On a grand scale, at least, chicanery required fluency, initiative, skepticism and wit—qualities which composed a *corriente* style of behavior townspeople admired, a style that contrasted with the solemn, gullible, and inarticulately timid manner they attributed to rustic folk.

By praising the variety of goods and services available in their town Mitleños acknowledged the fact that people benefited from making economic exchanges, but for the most part they assumed that one man's gains were another man's losses. We have already mentioned this point of view in describing the inclination of townspeople to tell and believe stories which accused wealthy people of having secured the aid of a devil. When roguery was involved in an economic exchange, and experience caused townspeople to think that this was a common possibility, then one person obviously benefited at the expense of someone else.

In sum, the society Mitleños looked out upon was largely an acquisitive society: monetary values colored most of their perceptions, they identified economic progress with the "civilization" of their community, and they considered the scramble for advantage in the market place to be a dominant element in their lives.

Yet, if we consider for a moment the Acquisitive Society Tawney described as one which, "by fixing men's minds, not upon the discharge of social obligations . . . but upon the exercise of the right to pursue their own self-interest . . . assures men that there are no ends other than their ends, no law other than their desires, no limit other than that which they think advisable," [5] and if we allow that such a society was suggested to townspeople by their experience in the market place, then we can appreciate their efforts to restrain and channelize a powerful element within their community.

Ideals of a Good Life

Perhaps societies encourage an obstinacy in human nature by making those acts most virtuous which are, in their particular scheme of things, most necessary and difficult to achieve. At any rate, we have already seen that in Mitla, where there were few institutional means for controlling violence, peacefulness was a supreme social value. Similarly, although townspeople complained that to labor was to suffer, and that one's most strenuous efforts came to naught when illness, drought, or some other misfortune intervened, they reserved their highest praise for the austere discipline of productive labor.

The man or woman who was married to a diligent worker was considered well-mated, and the admonition to be industrious fell easily from the lips of parents. Much prestige attached to wealth, and townspeople admired the sophistication of the facile entrepreneur, but the poorest and most humble individuals commanded the respect of the community if they were industrious.

Numerous virtues were associated with industry—patience, endurance, honesty, responsibility to kinsmen and community—which together composed the image of a serious and straightforward way of life. Respect for these virtues restrained individuals who were tempted to free-wheeling deviousness in the market place, just as it restrained the display of vanity and envy, the vices townspeople found most annoying.

When they were engaged in commercial transactions with individuals outside their intimate circle of *confianza,* and particularly with people with whom they were not even *conocido,* townspeople commonly appealed insincerely to ideals of honesty and generosity. But in their anecdotes about the market place they reserved their most comic effects for descriptions of the way rogues proclaimed their veracity and altruism. These anecdotes were cautionary tales which, besides teaching a realistic skepticism about human behavior, warned individuals that there were limits beyond which they could not go without making themselves ridiculous and contemptible.

Nevertheless, in the attempt to fashion their conduct after dignified notions of industriousness and generosity, most townspeople we knew ran head-on into their own limitations and the limitations of their society. "Thus is life!" they would exclaim in the course of describing the machinations of their fellows. And, as if there were no answer, they would ask, "What can one do?"

Individually and collectively they did what they could. There were formal methods of ensuring honesty. Thus, town officials arbitrated a continuous round of disputes over property, contracts, and petty economic transactions, and when they failed a litigant occasionally appealed to state officials. A merchant who loaned money or goods to men for trading journeys demanded written contracts, or kept the titles to his debtors' houses and lands as security. Even kinsmen sometimes recorded their important economic exchanges in writing.

Gossip, which exposed everyone's affairs to critical scrutiny, was especially quick to report breaches of confidence between friends or relatives. Such breaches in particular damaged a person's reputation, for they destroyed those relationships in which individuals found the greater part of their security and companionship. For those involved, the destruction was a catastrophe, and for others, a warning.

To strengthen relationships of confidence townspeople used the courtship of etiquette. They taught their children to curtsy and kiss the hands of their godparents and elder relatives, and, along with respectful terms of address, they continued this mode of greeting in adulthood. In addition, they proliferated the ritual obligations which bound them together by making extensive use of the Catholic institution of godparenthood, and by exchanging valuable gifts in the *guelagueza* system of mutual aid by which they financed festivals.

Townspeople meticulously counted and weighed and kept written records of the goods they ritually exchanged, but they showed the greatest deference when doing so. Even when we observed a notorious trick of the market place intrude upon a *guelagueza* exchange, the participants obstinately maintained the dignity of the occasion. In this instance the *mayordomo* of a saint's celebration received a turkey that had been gorged with water to increase its weight. When he hung it on a scale

73

by its feet to be weighed he pretended not to notice the water that ran from its beak and made a pool on the ground. However, he left the turkey on the scale for a considerable period of time, allowing the water to dribble over his foot while he courteously welcomed the guests who brought it. They, along with others present, avoided looking down.

Besides fortifying relationships of confidence between individuals, *guelagueza* exchanges helped them fulfill their obligations to the community. Townspeople frankly complained that the financial demands they made upon each other to sponsor saints' celebrations and to hold town offices were burdensome. We have described how piety was subordinated to the calculation of economic costs when they discussed the way *mayordomías* were arranged. However, gains made in the market place were given ethical value by being used as *guelagueza* and expended in service to the community. The requirements of these expenditures seemed irritatingly coercive to individuals as they labored to meet them, but when they imagined a society without them it was a society in which men acted as if there were "no law other than their desires, no limit other than that which they think advisable." The vision of this possibility inhibited would-be critics of the saints' festivals and caused them to go unheeded in the community at large.

Thus, familiar with the values of the market place, and priding themselves as experts at following its competitive ways, Mitleños nonetheless subordinated themselves and other members of their community to ideals of proper conduct which disabused all but the most obdurate individuals of the notion that they might live wholeheartedly in pursuit of their own self-interest.

The Market Place at the Cross

If we were to choose one occasion in the yearly round of Mitla on which townspeople collectively and most succinctly expressed their synthesis of commercial and non-commercial values, we would choose the ceremony on New Year's Eve when they went to a cross on the border of their town lands and petitioned for the things they wanted

74

during the coming year. Our friends said that the stone cross had been in that place longer than anyone could remember, but a few years before our stay in Mitla a wealthy merchant had built a small shrine to house it after vandals from a neighboring settlement had pulled it down. Like a boundary stone, the cross represented the integrity of their community to townspeople, and their pilgrimage to it possessed the hallowedness of tradition at the same time that it was a fashionable thing to do.

Beginning at dusk townspeople made their way individually and in small family groups to the barren hillside where the cross was located. As was customary on pilgrimages, individuals occasionally paused to pray as they placed an offering of stones in the branches of those plants which suggested a cross. According to Juan Matías, a typical prayer on this particular evening might be a petition of this sort: "I have come to ask for chickens, if you will give them to me. With God's aid, in another year I will have plenty of chickens. Now I am going to where there are more people to ask if by chance they have chickens to sell. So that I will have more chickens, I am going to buy a few. I will see if you have chickens to give me. I will see what each one costs."

Upon arriving at the shrine townspeople made similar petitions to the cross. Then they selected places in the vicinity and used articles they had brought from home, along with stray rocks, to build images of the things they wanted during the coming year: miniature fields of corn and maguey, corrals filled with pine cones to represent animals, and houses with small candles lighting their interiors. During the rest of the evening they ritualistically bought and sold these images, and ate and visited as they clustered around small fires. Individuals moved from group to group exchanging greetings and pretending to purchase the things they wanted in the coming year. They bargained pleasantly and completed their transactions with pebbles which they called the money of God.

Thus, on a hillside in the night at the beginning of a new year townspeople did not need to restrain their acquisitive impulses. In a ritual market place that was both solemn and gay they acted out the drama of buying and selling under auspices which fused the Acquisitive Society with the Good Society.

Epilogue

In large part our studies in the world view of Mitleños have turned upon two of their basic dilemmas: (1) the distance between their social ideals and the actualities of their society; (2) the incompatibility of some of their assumptions about the nature of the world and its goods.

We explored the first of these dilemmas most thoroughly in connection with the efforts of townspeople, in the face of constant discord, to maintain their image of Mitla as an open, peaceful community; and, again, in connection with their efforts to restrain those elements within their community which suggested an Acquisitive Society.

The second dilemma we described in greatest detail when we showed how townspeople were ensnarled by their doubts and fears about witchcraft, and by some of the beliefs and practices concerning the souls of the living and the dead. Even the episode at the cross, described in the last chapter, was marked by this characteristic ambivalence. After some American tourists had visited the ceremony, several Mitleños told us that some townspeople were ashamed to make their prayer images and conduct their sales in the presence of city people. Furthermore, a few townspeople, instead of participating in the ceremony at the cross, went to a nearby cave to pray for the things they wanted during the coming year. This was one of the caves which gossip described as a habitat of the devil-who-gave-wealth, and our acquaintances, suffering from ignorance or embarrassment, could not explain to us the full meaning, for those who engaged in it, of this annual visit to the cave. On New Year's

Eve, therefore, as on many other occasions, the townspeople we knew were discomfited by local beliefs and practices which they knew to be objects of incredulity or scorn among city people and some members of their own community.

But what we recorded in our final chapter about the social and integrative significance of the ceremony at the cross was more important to the townspeople we knew than the fact that they experienced much corrosive doubt and ambiguity. Despite everything, they achieved a sense of community and a view of life which combined casuistry with moral commitment. It was this achievement which was most characteristic of the world view of Mitleños, and which, for those of us who face in different cultural forms dilemmas similar to theirs, has a significance beyond their ken. Many townspeople combined humor and prudence, hedonism and gravity, worldliness and piety, and thus regarded their community as a sort of comedy of manners. They accustomed themselves to the conventions of lying, laughed at witchcraft, forgave themselves their vices, and enjoyed the fashionableness of their festivals. At the same time they sought the truth, feared witchcraft, worked hard to fulfill their communal obligations, and, in general, conducted themselves with respect for the opinions of their critical fellow townsmen.

The Comic Muse in Cultural Anthropology

In principle I believe that discussions of methodology in the social sciences are important, but who would deny that they are usually dull? In this respect most of us are like social reformers who dislike people, except that the situation is reversed—social science discussions of methodology often bore us because they are remote from people as we experience them.

Nevertheless, as I prepared this book for publication I was urged by friends whose advice I value to add to the introduction, or separately in an appendix, a full discussion of my methods of work. The advice seemed to me ponderous. I was happy, therefore, when Professor Eric Wolf read the manuscript and gave me his suggestions about what I might do. In part, he wrote:

> . . . The aspects of culture that you have chosen to report on present some methodological difficulties of observation as well as of reporting. The borderline between Art and Science (dignifying these two monsters with capitals for a moment) is here even more tenuous than usual. Some more could be said about this problem in your introduction than you do say now. It seems to me a point well worth elaborating upon, especially since future readers and reviewers will inevitably use it as a peg upon which to hang their impressions and reviews. The fact that the things you report on so rarely appear in any Middle American ethnography shows how uneasy people become when they must shift from things they can count or measure to things which they must attempt to grasp through empathy and insight. My sugges-

tion is simply that you may wish to defend yourself before the fact, should you wish to do so. Of course, you may not choose to do so, and insist simply that the work can stand on its own merits, as surely it can. I should sympathize with both attitudes.

I appreciate most in Professor Wolf's comment his calling Art and Science monsters, and his reference to the borderline between them. They are, of course, imaginary monsters, and the border between their realms is like an international boundary, fluctuating and arbitrary. Once more, there are chauvinists on both sides of the line. If some Humanists or Scientists (dignifying *these* two monsters with capitals for a moment) feel that what I have written is inhumane or unscientific, they will hardly be disarmed by a few additional paragraphs tucked into the introduction, or hidden away in the appendix.

Clearly, the idea of adding a methodological discussion to this work is not to address all future readers, but, as Professor Wolf very kindly puts it, to defend myself for writing about things which "rarely appear in any Middle American ethnography" because they must be learned "through empathy and insight." The words *empathy* and *insight* are praise words in contemporary anthropology, so the idea needs to be put more bluntly: this study of Mitla may get called unscientific. The present appendix is meant to contribute to the issue raised by such a characterization.

Thought about another way, Science and Art are not, after all, two monsters who rule adjacent lands with the boundaries jealously guarded by chauvinistic Scientists and Humanists; they are a single opposition, a metaphysical scarecrow left over from the Industrial Revolution. The clothes of this scarecrow may once have been quite respectable, but now their disconsolate flutter keeps only the most astigmatic birds pecking at distant edges of the field. Those with one form of astigmatism think that their lean pickings are *avant garde,* and those with another distortion claim that they are "on the growing edge of scientific knowledge." Let us light on the scarecrow's shoulder and survey cultural anthropology from the center of the field. We note one thing immediately—

80

The marketplace in Yalalag, a Zapotec town in the mountains north of Mitla.

The market fair at Santa Catarina honoring San Antonio, one of the most popular "pilgrimages" among Mitleños.

The interior of a Mitla household, with decorations and elaborate sand painting used in funeral ceremonies following burial.

the best scientific work is frequently the best literature. That is, it has qualities of both art and science: the desire to see things whole, the respect for the reader's sensibility, the close attention to empirical reality, and the reasoned argument.

Stuart Hampshire, an English philosopher, has written an article called "Can There Be a General Science of Man?" which begins with the following observation:

> One of the more elementary facts about sociology is that the literature of this science is very dull. This might not have been expected and calls for an explanation. The literature of social anthropology is far from dull. On the contrary, it is full of surprising and suggestive facts about human life. . . . One therefore opens a recommended book by an anthropologist with a pleasant expectation of learning something new and of finding methods related to results. By now, after all these years of methodological argument, one opens a work on sociology with a sigh and certainly with no pleasant expectation of coming across surprising and suggestive facts about human life.[1]

I have no idea what sociology books Mr. Hampshire has read, but I can guess the anthropology books he has had recommended to him. *Patterns of Culture? Magic, Science and Religion? The Golden Bough?* He is a Fellow at All Souls College, Oxford—*The Nuer?* or *The People of the Sierra?*

The point of this guessing game is that there are a number of books which, aside from their scientific contribution to the discipline of anthropology, are good reading. They form a distinct literature which can be enjoyed by a variety of educated people.

Even so, those of us who have read a great deal of anthropology can sympathize with E. R. Leach, who writes: "When I read a book by one of my anthropological colleagues, I am, I must confess, frequently bored by the facts."[2] We know, too, that much anthropology is poorly written. But this should not obscure the fact that from Frazer and Malinowski to such emerging writers as Julian Pitt-Rivers, W. R. Geddes and McKim Marriott, the literature of cultural anthropology has earned a substantial claim to the title of literature. So considered, the question naturally arises as to what the characteristic literary quality of this body of writing is and how this quality is related to the scientific or analytical intentions of the authors.

When we ask this question we discover that the patron deity of cultural anthropology is Thalia, the Comic Muse.

In the moment of our discovery numerous books spring to mind: the works of W. W. Howells, Earnest Hooton, Carlton Coon and Loren Eiseley; Elenore Smith Bowen's recent novel, *Return to Laughter;* fiction by Oliver Lafarge; the sketches of Alice Marriott; Kluckhohn's instructive and amusingly written *Mirror For Man.* We recall that in *The Golden Bough* Sir James Frazer examined what he called "the melancholy record of human error and folly," and that Lowie was often ironic—for example, his famous concluding paragraph to *Primitive Society,* with its often misconstrued Gilbert and Sullivan phrase about civilization being "a thing of shreds and patches."

But let us consider a single category of books in cultural anthropology: monographs which, like the present study of Mitleño world view, contribute directly to the science of anthropology by describing one or more whole cultures in some detail, and which are written in a manner that makes them available to a wide audience of educated people.

Since books are not written to fall into our categories, we do not need to agree upon how many books belong to this category, or upon their relative merits. Certainly, there are many books we could agree upon: *Argonauts of the Western Pacific; We, the Tikopia; The Chrysanthemum and the Sword; New Lives for Old; The Trumpet Shall Sound.* So striking is the literary quality of these titles that a non-anthropologist upon hearing them might guess that they were novels! But titles may be misleading. The reader who was attracted to *Penny Capitalism* by its title might well discover himself skipping over pages of detail about the average costs of chili and chicken coops in Guatemala. Despite its title, *Penny Capitalism* aims for less literary effect and a smaller audience than does, for example, *Amazon Town* by Charles Wagley.

Penny Capitalism, Nomads of the Long Bow, Empire's Children, Both Sides of Buka Passage, The Realm of a Rain Queen, Bantu Bu-

82

reaucracy are intended for smaller audiences than *Affable Savages, Growing Up in New Guinea* or *Nine Dyak Nights.* Yet the fashion of giving alliterative, romantic, even clever titles to monographs suggests the presence of one of the Classic Muses in cultural anthropology. The fashion does not admit funny titles like those which Earnest Hooton favored. Nor do we find within the covers of the books we are now discussing the type of humor that characterizes forthright popularizations. The Muse that presides over these books seldom provokes laughter, but allows many moods and encourages seriousness of purpose. In these respects she reminds us of Clio, the Muse of History, whom Trevelyan helped return to her place in the temple of the arts during the debacle of scientistic historiography.

That the Muse which inspires cultural anthropology is Thalia, the Comic Muse, can best be seen by examining her relationship to the analytical intentions of author anthropologists.

Ruth Benedict began *Patterns of Culture* with an analysis of ethnocentricism, particularly in the form of race prejudice. She concluded her argument this way:

> So modern man, differentiating into Chosen People and dangerous aliens, groups within his own civilization genetically and culturally related to one another as any tribes in the Australian bush are among themselves, has the justification of a vast historical continuity behind his attitude. The Pygmies have made the same claims.[3]

The ironic finesse with which these sentences link the prejudices of white racists to those of Pygmies, and the differences racists emphasize to the variations among Australian bushmen, reveals the skill of a first-rate comic writer.

One may protest that such sentences are no more than rhetorical flourishes incidental to the main argument of *Patterns of Culture.* I think not. The Comic Muse presides over Benedict's entire effort to make her reader see his own culture through the lens of knowledge of different cultures. The lens she provides her reader includes the Zuni, "incorri-

83

gibly mild" in contrast to the ecstatic Indians of the Plains; the prudish, suspicious and scheming Dobuan; the egomaniac Kwakiutl. They are related to what she calls "the great arc of human possibilities" in the same way that the characters created by such writers as Molière or Ben Jonson are related to human nature. Benedict's analysis belongs to the comedy of humors. Let Jonson speak:

> . . . so in every human body
> The choler, melancholy, phlegm, and blood,
> By reason that they flow continually
> In some one part, and are not continent,
> Receive the name of humours. *Now thus far*
> *It may by metaphor apply itself*
> *Unto the general disposition:*
> *As when some one peculiar quality*
> *Doth so possess a man that it doth draw*
> *All his affects, his spirits, and his powers,*
> *In their confluxions, all to run one way,*
> *This may be truly said to be a humour.*[4]

The impact of Ruth Benedict's book lies in her success in getting the reader to accept the notion that the total way of life of a people may be so dominated by "a humour," or what was later called "a ruling passion," that it appears insane when examined from a neutral, that is, non-ethnocentric, and I would now add comic, point of view.

Margaret Mead has employed a similar point of view in a distinguished series of books. The gracious Samoans, puritanical Manus Islanders, gentle Arapesh, fierce Mundugumor, contradictory Balinese, remain in our memory like characters from the novels of Charles Dickens or George Meredith. Mead never presents them as gesturing oddities, unrelated to ourselves. Her comparisons are quite direct. For example, in the first chapter of *Growing Up in New Guinea* she says that the world of the Manus Islanders "is . . . often . . . a weird caricature of our own, a world whose currency is shells and dogs' teeth, which makes its investments in marriages instead of corporations. . . ."[5]

84

Caricature is a comic mode. I do not mean to depreciate Margaret Mead's work by pointing to the fact that it is a mode she frequently employs. (Iatmul mothers, she writes, "stop their babies' temper tantrums by thrusting their nipples into their mouths like corks into soda-water bottles." [6])

Perhaps the books by Ruth Benedict and Margaret Mead which were intended for very large audiences will not be considered typical of cultural anthropology. But I find no less authority than Sir James Frazer, in his Introduction to *Argonauts of the Western Pacific,* comparing Malinowski's view of human nature to the views of Molière, Cervantes and Shakespeare.[7] (When Frazer included Shakespeare in this comparison he was undoubtedly thinking of Falstaff rather than Hamlet or Lear!)

Regardless of their influence upon other writers, unless the works of every giant are to be considered atypical, Malinowski's descriptions of the Trobriand Islanders must be considered in the mainstream of cultural anthropology. Who can forget the way *Argonauts of the Western Pacific* opens with a discussion of field methods in which the reader is told, "Imagine yourself suddenly set down surrounded by all your gear, alone on a tropical beach close to a native village, while the launch or dingy which has brought you sails away out of sight. . . . Imagine yourself then, making your first entry into the village. . . . Some natives flock round you, especially if they smell tobacco." [8] The Comic Muse presides over this form of writing.

Malinowski, Mead, Benedict, all belong to what has been called "the wind in the palm trees school of anthropology." The phrase identifies an important element in many books which portray cultures as wholes, use of what Kenneth Burke has called a "scene/act ratio." [9] By "scene/act ratio" is meant the meaningful relationship between an action and the physical scene in which it occurs. For example: when Lear goes mad on a heath at night during a storm the action and the setting in which it takes place are similar, but when a mystery writer brings a particularly sinister series of events to a climax in a sun-drenched meadow where sheep are contentedly grazing, the scene/act ratio plays upon our sense of incongruity.

The phrase, "wind in the palm trees . . . anthropology," insinuates that use of the scene/act ratio is inappropriate in scientific monographs. Yet Robert Redfield truly observed that Malinowski's invitation to us to leave the dusty library and follow him along the beach in the gathering twilight as natives collect around fires and tell stories, accomplishes a definite scientific purpose.[10] Malinowski was quite clear on this point. He asserted that anthropologists should write vividly in order to include within their analyses an aspect of reality which would otherwise be lost. He called this aspect of reality "the imponderabilia of actual life," and described it as consisting of "the tone of conversation . . . [the] passing sympathies and dislikes between people; the subtle yet unmistakable manner in which personal vanities and ambitions are reflected in the behaviour of the individual. . . ."[11] This is the same stuff that characterizes works of fiction which are traditionally called comedies of manners. Its role in cultural anthropology can be studied by analyzing the uses of metaphor and anecdote in many important monographs. Let us take a recent example, one that makes a most distinguished contribution to the science of anthropology, E. Adamson Hoebel's *The Law of Primitive Man*.

Hoebel uses metaphor and anecdote to describe such "imponderabilia of actual life" as "the immaturity" of the Comanches, who behaved with "the frenetic stridency of aggressive adolescents." On a Comanche war or raiding party, according to Hoebel, "at any point a man could pick up his arrows and go home." This lively paraphrase of the old saw, "he picked up his marbles and went home," sketches the comic figure of a childishly pouting warrior, and thus adds credibility to Hoebel's characterization of the Comanches' immaturity. In contrast, Hoebel says that the Cheyennes possessed "a sense of form, a feel for structured order, a maturity of emotion and action." And he illustrates this quality by anecdotes such as the reported behavior of a chief when he was interrupted during a ceremony to be informed that a man had absconded with his wife. The chief acted in what Hoebel says the Cheyennes considered an exemplary manner by returning to his ceremonial with the aloof comment, "A dog has pissed on my tent." [12]

Examples from Hoebel's book could be multiplied. The point to be made is that Hoebel has led the development within anthropology of an analytical scheme, the "legal realist" approach to trouble cases, which gives him great freedom to use the comic devices of literary anthropology. Without this freedom and the talent of a raconteur to exploit it fully, Hoebel could not have used the comparative method so boldly to combine a configurationalist sense of the cultural whole with a theory of progressive cultural evolution. This combination makes *The Law of Primitive Man* a landmark for the discipline of cultural anthropology.

Even the aspect of society which goes under the heading of social structure was described by Malinowski as possessing characteristics which we traditionally associate with the comedy of manners. Malinowski wrote that the anthropologist in presenting the anatomy of a society "gives us a picture of the natives subjected to a strict code of behaviour and good manners, to which in comparison the life at the Court of Versailles or Escorial was free and easy." [13]

This throws considerable light upon the monographs of such British anthropologists as Meyer Fortes, E. E. Evans-Pritchard, Raymond Firth, and Max Gluckman. Their studies are not concerned, in the way that many books by American anthropologists have been, with achieving a comic perspective upon our own culture, and the wind in their palm trees is no gale. Yet they aim for audiences wider than professional anthropologists, or even social scientists, and their contents are shaped with literary care to show us aspects of society which resemble in curious ways the stuff that goes into a Jane Austen novel.

This is not the place to draw meticulous distinctions between different kinds of comedy, and between different areas of cultural anthropology. I want simply to observe that we should study Bergson, Meredith, and other writers who have thought deeply upon the nature of comedy, in order to bring their thoughts to bear upon the literature of social anthropology. When we do we will speculate about the similarity of the preoccupations of anthropologists and comic novelists with the subtleties of kinship, marriage arrangements and status differences. Perhaps we will discover that some of the supposed scientific differences between the British and American "schools" of anthropology are differences between points of view derived from the comedy of manners on the one hand, and the comedy of humors on the other.

Some years ago when I was an anthropology student at the University of Chicago and had not yet undergone the mystic experience of field work, I remember hearing two students who were back from the field and full of their adventures discussing the way the people they had lived with gave spontaneous "Freudian" and "Durkheimian" and "Marxian" interpretations of various customs within their communities. They concluded, I believe, that natives were good "functionalists." The idea has obvious limitations, but for someone interested in world views it teases the imagination, for it gives a curious twist to the issue of how his own world view influences his perception of any other world view.

We have all heard that anthropologist A who described X society as paranoid is himself a little paranoid, and that anthropologist B who wrote about a bucolic society is at heart a Rousseauian. When I remember this, and the students who studied native communities whose members were "functionalists," I am troubled about our work in Mitla. Perhaps we and townspeople had what are called "compatible neuroses." We were very happy in Mitla.

And yet I cannot believe that wherever a man looks what he sees is primarily a reflection of himself. There is an ordered reality outside of ourselves, and one task of the artist and the scientist in each man is to search the relationships between the order which he sees in the world and the order which inheres in his act of seeing.

In our field work we tried to be good listeners, with all that this implies about not jumping to conclusions or imposing our own egos upon those we talked to. In addition, as I wrote the present study I carried on an imaginary dialogue with some of our Mitleño friends—in my imagination I explained to them what I was writing, and asked them what they thought about it. As a consequence I modified some of the things I was writing, making them, I believe, more accurate. I have already mentioned in the Introduction to this book that I wrote and discussed directly with townspeople while we were still in Mitla another manuscript describing their world view. Most of the events and practices described in the present book were in that earlier manuscript. Throughout my work I tried to record what some philosophers would call the "lived reality" of townspeople, so that they might recognize themselves and their community in what I wrote if it were told to them. In Malinowski's words, I sought to capture "the imponderabilia of actual life."

When we returned to the University of Chicago full of our adventures in the field, Professor Robert Redfield read my first manuscript. His criticisms were a profound lesson in scholarship, for he showed me that what I had written was repetitious of previous Mesoamerican ethnology, loosely argued, and unrelated to other scholarly work. Because some of the things I had written resembled some of the things in Huizinga's *The Waning of the Middle Ages,* he suggested that I read that book. What I found there helped me to write Chapter VI of this book.

For the next few years I searched the literature—Bergson, Tawney, Firth, Malinowski—looking for ways to connect our knowledge of Mitla to ideas in contemporary scholarship. The results are the other chapters of this book, which contain, I believe, three elements: information recorded by the naturalistic observation of human behavior (an element of history), connections seen between this information and the ideas of other students of human behavior (an element of science), and an attempt to communicate this information and these connections to a general audience of educated readers (an element of art). The last element is not less important than the first two, for the proper communication of scientific knowledge is essential to its existence.

Different modes of communication are, of course, appropriate and essential for different kinds of knowledge. The chairman of a sociology department once told me that he did not think a certain anthropological monograph was scientific. The book he named is famous among anthropologists as an exemplar of rigorous scientific analysis. The sociologist justified his opinion by pointing to the fact that there were no tables or charts in the monograph.

My thesis is that the Comic Muse in her various guises is the proper and traditional patron of a great part of the *scientific* literature of cultural anthropology.

Perched here on the scarecrow's shoulder I have only considered studies which describe one or more cultures as wholes and are written in a manner that makes them available to an audience wider than professional anthropologists. They are surely in the center of the field of cultural anthropology, but between them and stretching away in the distance are the long rows of professional journals, museum publications and other kinds of monographs which together account for a much larger proportion of anthropological writing than the books I have been considering.

At first glance it is a solemn scene. Here and there among these sober accumulations of knowledge we catch a glimpse of Thalia, but she seems now to be more a sprite hiding in the foliage than a patron deity of the grand manner.

Perhaps this first impression is misleading. Perhaps if we look closely we will see that an original impetus in the cultivation of the entire field is not so far from Thalia's ways as we suppose. Who can speak with more experience and authority on the history of the personality of anthropology than Alfred Louis Kroeber? Here is what he recently said:

> Since personalities are initially determined by their ancestry, it is a relevant fact, if I am right, that anthropology was originally not a social science at all. Its father was natural science; its mother, esthetically tinged humanities. Both parents want to attain reasoned and generalized conclusions; but they both also want to reach them by way of their senses as well as by reasoning. After a brief first childlike

decade or two of outright speculation, anthropology settled down to starting directly from experienced phenomena, with a bare minimum of ready-made abstraction and theory, but with a glowing conviction that it was entering new territory and making discovery. Its discovery was consciousness of the world of culture, an enormous product and a vast influence, with forms and patterns of its own, and a validating principle: relativity. There were far boundaries to this demesne, which included in its totality alike our own and the most remote and diverse human productivities. The vision was wide, charged, and stirring. It may perhaps fairly be called romantic: certainly it emerged historically about at the time point when esthetic romanticism was intellectualizing. The pursuit of anthropology must often have seemed strange and useless to many people, but no one has ever called it an arid or a toneless or a dismal science.

Now, maturity has stolen upon us. The times and utilitarianism have caught up with us, and we find ourselves classified and assigned to the social sciences. It is a dimmer atmosphere, with the smog of jargon sometimes hanging heavy. Generalizations no longer suffice; we are taught to worship Abstraction; sharp sensory outlines have melted into logicoverbal ones. As our daily bread, we invent hypotheses in order to test them, as we are told is the constant practice of the high tribe of physicists. If at times some of you, like myself, feel somewhat ill at ease in the house of social science, do not wonder: we are changelings therein; our true paternity lies elsewhere.

I do not end on a note of despondency; for the routes of fulfillment are many. And specifically, it is well that with all their differences of habitus, of attitude, of kinds of building stones, sociology and anthropology have emerged with a substantially common basic theory. That should be an encouragement to both, and a rallying point to others. And it will serve as a foundation for all the social sciences to build on.[14]

Our study of Mitla has been an effort to contribute one more anthropological stone to the house of social science of which Kroeber speaks.

Notes

Introduction

1. Robert Redfield, *The Primitive World and Its Transformations*, p. 87.
2. Robert Redfield, *The Little Community: Viewpoints for the Study of a Human Whole*, p. 95.
3. Morris Swadesh, "El Idioma de los Zapotecos."
4. Elsie Clews Parsons, *Mitla, Town of the Souls*.

Chapter I.

1. Parsons, *Mitla*, pp. xii–xiii.
2. *Ibid.*, pp. xi–xii.
3. Sol Tax, *Penny Capitalism: A Guatemalan Indian Economy*, p. 12.
4. Parsons, *Mitla*, p. 445.
5. *Ibid.*, p. 400.
6. *Ibid.*, pp. 54–60.
7. *Ibid.*, p. 535.
8. *Ibid.*, pp. 20, 21.
9. Lionel Trilling, *The Liberal Imagination*, p. 201.
10. Raymond Firth, *Elements of Social Organization*, p. 31.
11. Julio de la Fuente, *Yalalag, Una Villa Zapoteca Serrana*, p. 22. See also by the same author, "Los Zapotecas de Choapan, Oaxaca."
12. See Chapter VI, "The Souls and the Saints," where we describe disagreements between townspeople about the *mayordomías*, and the secular character of these festivals. We are not here assuming that Mitla was an ideally integrated community. Since, however, the *mayordomías* in Mitla and in neighboring towns were a traditional part of their systems of town

service, were cooperatively financed by gift exchanges, and were given in honor of community-owned images of saints, we feel justified in assuming that they contributed to social solidarity, and that variation in the number of *mayordomías* in these communities was *one* important index of their *relative* integration.

13. Parsons, *Mitla*, p. 10.

14. Town officials organized and directed these censuses in order to report to the federal government on the literacy of townspeople. We observed the census of 1953 and believe that it was fairly reliable. We learned that it was going to be made too late to give instruction to all of the census takers to ask about the languages spoken by the townspeople, but we did get them to collect enough information to make the following reasonable estimate:

	Per cent of total population
Zapotec speaking	90
Spanish speaking	70
Zapotec and Spanish bilingual	60
Zapotec monolingual	30
Spanish monolingual	10

The 1940 national census of Mexico was used by Professor Manuel Germán Parra to compile the monograph *Densidad de la población de habla indígena en la república Méxicana*. That work records the population of the *municipio* of Mitla as 4,799, with 65 per cent Zapotec speaking (35 per cent bilingual Zapotec and Spanish speaking, 30 per cent Zapotec monolinguals), and 35 per cent Spanish speaking monolinguals. These figures include the Spanish monolingual settlements of Xaagá and Loma Larga. In 1953, however, the total population of Loma Larga was 146 individuals, and that of Xaagá only slightly larger, so that the total population of the *municipio* of Mitla in 1953 was considerably less than the 4,799 shown in the 1940 census. Although Xaagá and Loma Larga may have undergone a radical depopulation between 1940 and 1953, we are inclined to think that the 1940 census was in error. At any rate, Mitleños did not consider these settlements to be a part of their community.

15. Alejandro Marroquín, *Tlaxiaco, una ciudad mercado*, p. 85.

Chapter II.

1. Bronislaw Malinowski, *Magic, Science and Religion and Other Essays,* p. 146.
2. Parsons, *Mitla,* pp. 209–210, 363–364.
3. No one admitted to us having gone to the caves for the purpose of making any kind of petition, but when we visited the caves ourselves we found candles, bits of paper and other objects which had been used in rituals. In the Epilogue to the present book, we record the fact that a few townspeople made a pilgrimage to one of these caves on New Year's Eve. Our Mitleño friends did not believe that the people who went to the cave at that time went to petition the devil, but they did maintain, and from our general knowledge of the community we believe correctly, that some individuals, hoping and at the same time fearing that the devil contract stories were true, actually sought the aid of the devil at these places.
4. In the dialect of the town this devil was called *ben dzaab,* ugly person, and he was described as having a white skin and heavy beard, and dark clothing in the style of city people.
5. Parsons, *Mitla,* pp. 15–16.
6. *Ibid.,* pp. 166–168.
7. Malinowski, *Magic,* p. 136.
8. E. R. Leach, *Political Systems of Highland Burma.*
9. *Ibid.,* p. 278.
10. Samuel Taylor Coleridge, *Coleridge's Miscellaneous Criticism,* pp. 435–436.
11. This tradition was known and at least partially believed in towns as far away as Yalalag, where a dialect of Zapotec was spoken that was unintelligible to Mitleños.
12. Parsons, *Mitla,* pp. 324–364. See also Parsons, "Zapoteca and Spanish Tales of Mitla, Oaxaca."
13. For example, in 1932 Parsons wrote, ". . . Had I not returned for a second visit to Mitla I would have been persuaded that no Indian folktale had survived in this rapidly modernizing town. . . . Then on my second visit we found Miguel Mendez . . . and heard his tales of Sus Ley and Lightning . . . and Miguel told them too like an Indian, as if he believed them. I don't think he questioned that the Old Ones who

built Las Ruinas went underground. . . . When Miguel was telling this . . . I could hear a Pueblo Indian of New Mexico tell of spirit animals. . . ."—Parsons, "Zapoteca," pp. 277–278.
14. Reed Whittemore, "Churchill and the Limitations of Myth," p. 262.

Chapter III.
1. Alfred North Whitehead, *The Aims of Education*, p. 40.
2. Parsons, *Mitla*, pp. 443–444.
3. *Ibid.*, pp. 480, 481.
4. *Ibid.*, p. 493.
5. Jerome Frank, as quoted by E. Adamson Hoebel, *The Law of Primitive Man*, pp. 29–30.
6. Parsons, *Mitla*, p. 481, footnote 5. This two-sentence footnote is an amusing example of Parsons' method in what we have called her "portrait" of Mitla. It is a footnote to her statement that townspeople "fear . . . making enemies," and reads in full: "This is probably based on fear of the injury your enemy can work supernaturally. Quiche rituals against enemies are certainly fear-inspiring (Bunzel)." Mitleños did not have knowledge of or contacts with Quiché-speaking towns, and Parsons did not say why Mitleños might fear witchcraft because villagers in Guatemala had fearful rituals, but she led the reader to this inference, and seems to have made it herself.
7. *Ibid.*, pp. 167–168.

Chapter IV.
1. Charles Baudelaire, *The Essence of Laughter*, pp. 117–118.
2. Parsons, *Mitla*, p. 17.
3. *Ibid.*, p. 426.
4. Professor Redfield, in his comparative analysis of four communities in Yucatan, has discussed the uncertainty among town and city folk of the causes of illnesses. He found that the frequency with which people thought that they suffered from black magic and their anxiety that it might be used against them was greatest "in the town and city, where some people are skeptical of the reality of witchcraft" and least in the communities where "belief is least challenged."—Robert Redfield, *The Folk Culture of Yucatan*, p. 334, and Chapter XI, "Medicine and

Magic," *passim*. Our understanding of witchcraft in Mitla has been greatly aided by Redfield's analysis of social change in Yucatan.

5. George Meredith, "An Essay on Comedy."
6. Henri Bergson, "Laughter," p. 187.
7. *Ibid.*, pp. 178, 73–74.
8. These nicknames combined Spanish and Zapotec words, or were simply Spanish words given a local pronunciation. In Spanish the names in the following sentence were: *pie de camarón, tortuga, catrina, diente de marimba, chico cuchi,* but they were usually pronounced *nirs camaron', tortū', catrin, dient marim, chico chūc;* the word which we have translated *Big Testicles* was *balaños*. Our Mitleño friends explained its significance to us. The dictionary contains *bálano,* meaning the glans of the penis, from which the nickname *balaños* may be derived.
9. Bergson, "Laughter," pp. 169, 170.
10. Juan's nickname was the Zapotec name of a parasite that burrows into the feet; he was also known in Spanish as "Rag." Both nicknames referred to his poverty.
11. Bergson, "Laughter," p. 71.
12. *Ibid.*, p. 71.

Chapter V.

1. Redfield, *Yucatan,* p. 237.
2. *Muina,* or *mohina,* an illness caused by intense anger, was frequently mentioned by townspeople. It was usually an affliction of adults, but the notion that a mother's *muina* would poison her milk was common. When one of our neighbors got in an argument with her brothers she said that they would be responsible for the death of her baby if it sickened from the *muina* that was liable to infect her milk. The symptoms of *muina* were diarrhea, fever, headaches and stomach aches.
3. This is the version of Severiano's death that the marimba players brought back to Mitla.
4. Parsons, *Mitla,* pp. 529–530, 535.
5. *Ibid.*, p. 530.
6. *Ibid.*, p. 511.
7. The Spanish words for sin and sinner were loan words in the Zapotec dialect of Mitla. Mitleños used a great many Spanish loan words in ordinary conversation as well as in formal speeches in Zapotec. Both Paul

Radin and Morris Swadesh have commented on the large number of Spanish loan words in Zapotec dialects. See Paul Radin, "A Preliminary Sketch of the Zapotec Language"; Swadesh, "El Idioma," pp. 415–448.

Chapter VI.

1. Malinowski, *Magic,* p. 146.
2. Johan Huizinga, *The Waning of the Middle Ages,* p. 151.
3. Parsons, *Mitla,* pp. 362–363. Considering the import of the story as a whole, the version recorded by Parsons concluded with sanctimonious aplomb, "From this we know that the souls live in the same house with us."
4. Pedro Santiago dictated this prayer to me in Spanish when I asked him how he or some other townsman would address the souls in prayers. We asked this same question of several other townspeople and they told us similar prayers. We recorded a few texts of prayers and formalities of speech for special occasions in the Zapotec dialect of townspeople. Miss Eleanor Briggs of the Summer Institute of Linguistics had mastered the dialect of Mitla and she kindly corrected and translated our transcriptions. These prayers, too, were similar to the one quoted above.
5. Huizinga, *Middle Ages,* p. 167.

Chapter VII.

1. R. H. Tawney, *The Acquisitive Society,* p. 29.
2. Parsons, *Mitla,* p. 445.
3. *Ibid.,* pp. 12–13.
4. Mitleños called this malady *antojos.* George Foster identifies it, along with other illnesses caused by strong emotional experiences (*susto, colerina, pispelo,* etc.), as characteristic of Hispanic American folk medicine.—George M. Foster, "Relationships Between Spanish and Spanish-American Folk Medicine."
5. Tawney, *The Acquisitive Society,* pp. 30–31.

Appendix

1. Stuart Hampshire, "Can There Be a General Science of Man?" p. 164.
2. Leach, *Political Systems,* p. 227.
3. Ruth Benedict, *Patterns of Culture,* pp. 7–8.

4. Ben Jonson, Induction to *Everyman out of his Humour* (1599–1600). Quoted in L. J. Potts, *Comedy,* p. 119.
5. Margaret Mead, *Growing up in New Guinea,* p. 10.
6. Margaret Mead, *Male and Female,* p. 59.
7. James Frazer, Introduction to Bronislaw Malinowski, *Argonauts of the Western Pacific,* p. ix.
8. Malinowski, *Argonauts,* p. 4.
9. Kenneth Burke, *A Grammar of Motives,* pp. 3–7.
10. Robert Redfield, Introduction to Bronislaw Malinowski, *Magic, Science and Religion and Other Essays,* pp. 9–13.
11. Malinowski, *Magic,* pp. 18–22.
12. Hoebel, *Primitive Man,* p. 160.
13. Malinowski, *Argonauts,* p. 10.
14. A. L. Kroeber, "The History of the Personality of Anthropology," p. 404.

Literature Cited

Baudelaire, Charles. *The Essence of Laughter*. New York: Meridian Books, 1956.

Benedict, Ruth. *Patterns of Culture*. Boston: Houghton Mifflin Co., 1934.

Bergson, Henri. "Laughter." In *Comedy*. Wylie Sypher, editor. Garden City, N.Y.: Doubleday Anchor Books, 1956.

Burke, Kenneth. *A Grammar of Motives*. New York: Prentice-Hall, 1945.

Coleridge, Samuel Taylor. *Coleridge's Miscellaneous Criticism*. Thomas Middleton Raysor, editor. London: Constable and Co., 1936.

De la Fuente, Julio. "Los Zapotecas de Choapan, Oaxaca." *Anales del Instituto Nacional de Antropología e Historia*. II (1941–46), 143–205. Mexico, 1947.

———. *Yalalag, Una Villa Zapoteca Serrana*. Mexico: Serie Científica 1, Museo Nacional de Antropología, Instituto Nacional de Antropología e Historia, 1949.

Firth, Raymond. *Elements of Social Organization*. London: Watts & Co., 1951.

Foster, George M. "Relationships Between Spanish and Spanish-American Folk Medicine." *Journal of American Folklore*, LXVI (1953), 201–217.

Frazer, James. Introduction to Bronislaw Malinowski, *Argonauts of the Western Pacific*. London: George Routledge, 1922.

Germán Parra, Manuel. *Densidad de la población de habla indígena en la república Méxicana*. Memorias del Instituto Nacional Indigenista. Vol. 1, No. 1. Mexico, 1950.

Hampshire, Stuart. "Can There Be a General Science of Man?" *Commentary*, XXIV (1957), 164.

Hoebel, E. Adamson. *The Law of Primitive Man.* Cambridge: Harvard University Press, 1954.

Huizinga, Johan. *The Waning of the Middle Ages.* Garden City, N.Y.: Doubleday Anchor Books, 1954.

Kroeber, Alfred Louis. "The History of the Personality of Anthropology." *American Anthropologist,* LXI (1959), 398–404.

Leach, E. R. *Political Systems of Highland Burma.* Cambridge: Harvard University Press, 1954.

Malinowski, Bronislaw. *Argonauts of the Western Pacific.* London: George Routledge, 1922.

———. *Magic, Science and Religion and Other Essays.* Garden City, N.Y.: Doubleday Anchor Books, 1954.

Marroquín, Alejandro. *Tlaxiaco, una ciudad mercado.* Mexico: Instituto Nacional Indigenista, 1954.

Mead, Margaret. *Growing Up in New Guinea.* New York: William Morrow, 1930.

———. *Male and Female.* New York: Mentor Books, 1955.

Meredith, George. "An Essay on Comedy." In *Comedy.* Wylie Sypher, editor. Garden City, N.Y.: Doubleday Anchor Books, 1956.

Parsons, Elsie Clews. "Zapoteca and Spanish Tales of Mitla, Oaxaca." *Journal of American Folklore,* XLV (1932), 277–317.

———. *Mitla, Town of the Souls.* Chicago: University of Chicago Press, 1936.

Potts, L. J. *Comedy.* London and New York: Hutchinson's University Library, 1948.

Radin, Paul. "A Preliminary Sketch of the Zapotec Language." *Language,* VI (1930), 64–85.

Redfield, Robert. *The Folk Culture of Yucatan.* Chicago: University of Chicago Press, 1941.

———. Introduction to Bronislaw Malinowski, *Magic, Science and Religion and Other Essays.* Garden City, N.Y.: Doubleday Anchor Books, 1954.

———. *The Primitive World and Its Transformations.* Ithaca: Cornell University Press, 1953.

———. *The Little Community: Viewpoints for the Study of a Human Whole.* Chicago: University of Chicago Press, 1955.

——— and Sol Tax. "General Characteristics of Present-Day Mesoamerican

Indian Society." In *Heritage of Conquest*. Sol Tax, editor. Glencoe, Ill.: The Free Press, 1952.

Swadesh, Morris. "El Idioma de los Zapotecos." In *Los Zapotecos: Monografía Histórica, Etnográfica y Económica*. Lucio Mendieta y Núñez, editor. Mexico: Universidad Nacional Autónoma de México, 1949.

Tawney, R. H. *The Acquisitive Society*. New York: Harcourt, Brace and Co., Harvest Books, n.d.

Tax, Sol. *Penny Capitalism: A Guatemalan Indian Economy*. Washington: Smithsonian Institution, Institute of Social Anthropology, Publication No. 16, 1953.

Trilling, Lionel. *The Liberal Imagination*. Garden City, N.Y.: Doubleday Anchor Books, 1953.

Whitehead, Alfred North. *The Aims of Education*. New York: Mentor Books, 1949.

Whittemore, Reed. "Churchill and the Limitations of Myth." *Yale Review*, XLIV (1955), 248–263.

Index

Edited by Georgiana W. Strickland
Designed by Sylvia Winter
Set in Linotype Granjon and Masterman display
Printed on Warren's Olde Style Antique Wove
Bound in Schlossers Elephant Hide paper
Manufactured in the United States of America